THE 12 SPHERES OF LEADERSHIP

12 TYPES OF LEADERS
THAT SHAPE THE DESTINIES OF NATIONS

GREATNESS
PUBLISHING

ANDRE THOMAS

http://www.12slm.org

Published by Greatness Publishing, Ontario, Canada

Cover design by Farouk Roberts,

Library and Archives Canada
ISBN 978-0986887857

All Scripture quotations are from the New King James Version of the Bible, except otherwise stated.

DEDICATION

I dedicate this book to Bishop Dr. David Oyedepo for being a model spiritual leader and father to multitudes. Your example, ministry of the word, and prayer for me rescued my greatness.

ACKNOWLEDGEMENTS

I wish to thank the leaders and members of
Divine Visitation Assemblies for their prayers and support
for the completion of this book.

Thanks to the editorial team of Heather Thane, Cathy–Ann Forde and
Valarie Akujobi.

Thanks to Avenella Griffith for the finishing editing touch you put on
this book project.

Thanks to my beloved wife Prophetess Nina for your prayers and
support of this book and the vision.

I also want to thank my Lord Jesus Christ for entrusting me with this
revelation of the *12 Spheres of Leadership that shape the destinies of
nations.*

A big thank you to the Holy Spirit who anointed me to finish this
project in very challenging times. You are more than enough.

TABLE OF CONTENTS

Chapter 17

INTRODUCTION

There are five major ways fresh revelation comes to a servant of the Lord:

1. Personal study of the scriptures.
2. Making enquiries of God to answer nagging questions.
3. The school of experience.
4. The preaching and teaching of other men and women of God.
5. A revelation given by divine sovereignty.

The revelation on the 12 Spheres of Leadership came to me by divine sovereignty in the form of a dream. I believe that the entrance of this word will bring illumination to the eyes of your understanding. It will bring wisdom that will ignite your vision and unlock the best version of you. It will help you uncover your latent gifts and empower you to become the greatest version of yourself.

As you read this book, expect to receive an encounter with the wisdom of God. Divine Wisdom is thinking thoughts, applying principles and taking steps to create what God desires. You were not put in a world that was wired for your failure. Your precious Heavenly Father put you in the world that is prepared for your gifts, uniqueness, and solutions.

I believe that as you read this book, the greatest version of you will emerge and you will impact your world.

CHAPTER 1

UNDERSTANDING LEADERSHIP

Leadership is using influence to work with and through people to fulfill a vision. The human spirit contains gifts from God while the soul contains passion and competence. Leaders have ideas on how the future should be and use various methods of influence to unlock the innate gifting, passion and competence of people to take their ideas from concept to reality.

Leadership is in its purest form the application of influence to fulfill a vision. Leadership is required when a vision requires the participation of more than one person for its fulfillment. However, leadership is not required when another person is not involved. Due to the fact that every significant vision on earth will require the participation of more than one person, leadership is required to bring significant visions from concept to reality.

Vision is the birthplace of leadership. It is the fountain that produces the need for leadership. It is a clear mental portrait of a preferred future. It is a picture of what the future looks like if we maximize the potential of a person or a people. Truly, as the scriptures state in Proverbs 29:18, "Without a vision, the people perish." It is also a truth

1

that without good leadership significant visions perish.

When we look at the first portrait that God paints of Himself on the canvas of our minds and hearts, using the paintbrush of the scriptures, we see a God who introduces Himself to mankind as a visionary who created His vision. It was stated in Genesis 1:1 that, "In the beginning, God created the heavens and the earth." He first had a vision, which was a mental portrait of a heaven and earth and then He created it.

With reference to Genesis 1:6, God had His most significant vision when He said, "Let Us make man." What is striking is that when he used the words, "let Us," the vision was for a product or creature called 'man' to be created in the image and likeness of God. However, it took the team of the Father, Son and Holy Ghost to fulfil the said vision. This illustrates that even the Godhead operates in a leadership team structure.

Man was made in the image and likeness of God who operated as a visionary and who worked with other beings like Himself, to create a future that He desired. Whether or not you like the title 'leader' or the mere thought of being a leader is undesirable, you are a leader because you were made in the image and likeness of a leader.

In order for you to fulfill God's plan for your life, you will need to do what your Creator does. He has a clearly defined future that He desires, and He works with spiritual beings just like Himself in teamwork and cooperation to create that future.

There are many concepts and ideologies about Leadership. Indeed, it is one of the most thought about, talked about, researched, and debated subjects on the earth. However, the greatest book on the subject of Leadership is the book that was written by the greatest leader of all, our Heavenly Father, the One whose Leadership vision included you and me.

There are different Leadership approaches and while doing my research, I have identified three distinct Leadership Ideologies: the Commonwealth Leadership Ideology, the Emperor Leadership Ideology and the Transactional Leadership Ideology.

COMMONWEALTH LEADERSHIP IDEOLOGY

The Biblical Ideology which was demonstrated in Ephesians 2:12 is the Commonwealth Leadership Ideology. This leadership style exercised influence for the increase of the common wealth of a group of people. It shaped the future with ideas so that those under its influence would increase in wealth, progress, breakthroughs, and all things good. Moses, Joshua, David, Solomon, Nehemiah, Deborah, Esther, Paul and Peter exercised the Commonwealth Leadership Ideology.

This leadership was exemplified in the Book of Joshua, where Joshua while leading the people into the Promised Land took the cities of Jericho and Ai. As a result, soon after that, every tribe was activated by the common victory to pursue and occupy their own territory.

This type of leadership finds its joy in increasing the quality of life of the people under its care. Its joy is not in the individual gift, influence or wealth of the leader. It is in how that leader uses his/her gifts, knowledge, and wealth to increase the collective influence, wealth and happiness of the people under their care. This leadership theory focuses on others. It is the way of the servant leader and is very different from the next leadership style.

EMPEROR LEADERSHIP IDEOLOGY

The Emperor Leadership Ideology states that the people that are under the influence of the leader exist only to create a platform for that leader's ambition. They are mobilized, manipulated if necessary, and forced if required, only to sustain, protect and advance the throne of the emperor. The subjects of that influence are simply what petrol is to a car – human fuel. This theory sees people as expendable with the same value as petrol.

TRANSACTIONAL LEADERSHIP IDEOLOGY

Transactional Leadership Ideology is based on two notions; 'I scratch my back and you scratch my back' or 'I have $20 to give you for a n hour of work and only if you produce that work, then will I give you $20.' There is no loyalty involved; its only motivation is characterized by the value of the transaction. This leadership style is used around the world and is certainly better than the Emperor style because at least you get something; but it does not lend for the greatness of people to emerge.

In this book, we will focus on the **Commonwealth Leadership Ideology** which is also referred to as **'Servant Leadership.'**

Let's look at some examples of people using the three different ideologies:

MOSES: A COMMONWEALTH LEADER

The Lord God instructed Moses in Exodus 3:19-22 to lead the people out of Egypt and He ensured that they did not leave Egypt empty-handed. He wanted them to gain something under Moses' leadership so that not only was he required to deliver the people, but they were to be profited in the initial stages.

The people of Israel would have been grateful to Moses for just delivering them out of slavery but the fact that they prospered financially during the process was an added bonus. This occurred because the Commonwealth Ideology that God and Moses operated caused Moses to bring the people into profit. This is very different from the ideology of many leaders who say 'I don't want the people to profit, I want myself to profit; they exist for my profit'. A commonwealth leader leads for the profit of the people under his influence.

SAUL: AN EMPEROR LEADER

In 1 Samuel 14:20-30, 43-45, Jonathan partners with God in his capacity as a military leader and brings about a victory against the enemies of Israel. He was also a game changer. Saul made a stupid oath based on his emotions and not his intellect – that no man should eat food that day even after fighting. His son, Jonathan came in, and after leading a great victory, tastes a little honey.

His father, upon discovering this in the aftermath of the battle, was determined to have him killed because he broke the oath that he did not know or hear about. It is obvious that in the value system of Saul, his son Jonathan – his military champion – was expendable. He was simply human fuel to Saul and the gift of gratitude and appreciation for Jonathan's exploits was non-existent.

An emperor leader shows no appreciation, gratitude, or loyalty and even after a person makes a great contribution that has changed the fortunes of a team, city or nation, he/she is considered expendable. You are just another a candle that has given its light. Now, bring the next candle, please.

BALAK: A TRANSACTIONAL LEADER

In Numbers 22-24, Balak, King of Moab, who feared that the approaching children of Israel had military might to overthrow him and seize his territory, proceeded to hire Balaam for a sum of money to prophesy against the children of Israel. That was a transaction.

Balaam and Balak did not share the same vision or loyalties. It was simply a transaction. The only influence that Balak had over Balaam was the influence of the money being offered, and the only influence that Balaam had on Balak was the possible evil use of the prophetic gift in him to curse Israel.

Now that we have laid the foundation of leadership ideology, let's look at how leaders shape the destinies of nations with their ideas and actions.

CHAPTER 2

UNDERSTANDING THE DESTINIES OF NATIONS

In Scripture, the Spirit of God reveals the mystery of personal and national greatness. Every individual can aspire to greatness because it is God's call on every person's life. How can greatness be expressed through you? God's plan for individual greatness requires you to:

1. Become one who fulfills their destiny in Christ and successfully serves God-given solutions to others.
2. Become the best version of yourself.

"And I saw no temple in it, for the Lord God Almighty is its temple, even the Lamb. And the city had no need of the sun, nor of the moon, that they might shine in it, for the glory of God illuminated it, and its lamp is the Lamb. And the nations of those who are saved will walk in the light of it; and the kings of the earth bring their glory and honor into it. And its gates may not be shut at all by day, for there shall be no night there. And they shall bring the glory and honor of the nations into it. And there shall in no way enter into it anything that defiles, or any making an abomination or a lie; but only those

who are written in the Lamb's Book of Life (Revelation 21:22-27). *"*
"What is man that you are mindful of him, and the son of man, that
you visit him? For you have made him lack a little from God, and have
crowned him with glory and honor. You made him rule over the works
of your hands; you have put all things under his feet: all sheep and
oxen, yes, and the beasts of the field; the birds of the heavens and
the fish of the sea, and all that pass through the paths of the seas. O
Jehovah, our Lord, how excel- lent is your name in all the earth
(Psalm 8:4-9)*!"*

Personal greatness is revealed in Psalm 8:4-8. This text declares that
when God made man, He crowned Him with glory and honor in
the following ways:

The person's 'crown' gives them the capacity and authority to lead in
that arena. This 'crown' is God's deposit of glory in the person.

The glory of God in a person is the aspect of divinity in a person that
comes in the form of an uncommon gift – a gift that makes the person
uncommon (or unique and needed) when it is developed and served.

Second, honour is a person's God-given authority, innate value and
solution (purpose).

When a person is ignorant of their God-given innate glory and honour,
they cannot "put on their crown," and function in the anointing and
purpose to which God has called them. Since they cannot "put on their
crown," they cannot advance – reign in life and be the "head and
not the tail," or succeed – be above only and not beneath.

This God-given innate glory and honour combination is a
person's greatness.

UNDERSTANDING THE DESTINIES OF NATIONS

There is more about this subject in my book; *"**Unlock Your Greatness**"*. In Revelation 21:26 God has not only given glory and honour to individuals, He has also given them to nations. This Scripture brings to light the following truths:

- In eternity, the glory and honour of nations will be celebrated.
- God has put an aspect of Himself, called His glory, into every nation.
- Every nation has been given a unique honour and value among the other nations.
- The greatness of a nation is its manifested glory and honour.
- Every nation has a unique expression of divinity among its people, and a purpose expressed as a unique, divine solution to serve the world's needs if it follows God's program.

The greatness of a nation will not emerge if the greatness of its leaders does not emerge; the glory and honour of a nation will never emerge if the glory and honour of its leaders does not emerge.

Heaven celebrates the manifestation of the glory and honour of leaders and nations.

Different types of leaders must manifest their personal glory and honour for the greatness of a nation to emerge. Your nation, irrespective of the circumstances in which it finds itself, has God-given glory and honour hidden in its destiny. Satan's goal is to block its manifestation. He uses his leaders in their various categories, including political leaders to achieve his goal. God's agenda for the manifestation of the glory and honour of nations is found in the release of the glory and honour of its leaders. Let us study this deeper.

"I say the truth in Christ, I lie not, my conscience also bearing me

witness in the Holy Ghost, that I have great heaviness and continual sorrow in my heart. For I could wish that I myself were accursed from Christ for my brethren, my kinsmen according to the flesh: Who are Israelites; to whom pertaineth the adoption, and the glory, and the covenants, and the giving of the law, and the service of God, and the promises; Whose are the fathers, and of whom as concerning the flesh Christ came, who is over all, God blessed forever. Amen (Romans 9:1-5)."

In studying the evolution of nations, it is realized that all nations came from Noah and his three sons Shem, Ham and Japheth (see Genesis 10). Genesis 11 states that they all spoke the same language and had "one speech." Together they decided to build a tower that would reach the heavens. This they determined to do in their own name, not in the name of God, their Creator.

God saw their plan and stopped the project, giving each nation its own language. He then called Abram (see Genesis 12) and gave him an assignment to create a model nation. Through this model nation, God intended to bless all the other nations of the earth. His dealings with this nation would showcase how He would deal with other nations, and this nation would become a light to all nations of the world. The glory and honour of the model nation, Israel, is unique.

In the first few chapters of the book of Exodus, Israel is in bondage as a nation. The Hebrew people were serving Egypt as slaves both physically and economically. However, in the womb of that oppressed nation was its glory and honour. Israel's glory and honour is identified in Romans 9:4-5. To Israel, belongs the model, which can be broken down as follows:

Adoption: The process for being adopted into the family of God was revealed to Israel and through Israel to the world.

The glory: The nature of the glory of God was revealed to Israel in the events described in the book of Exodus, and through Israel in the ministry of Jesus to the world.

The covenants: The old covenant and the new covenant were revealed to Israel and through Israel to the world.

The giving of the law: The law found in the Old Testament with its rules and regulations was given to Israel and through Israel to the world.

The service of God: The protocol, process and qualifications for serving God as a priest, king and servant were given to Israel and through Israel to the world.

The promises: God's general promises to mankind were revealed to Israel and through Israel to the world.

The fathers: The fathers of the faith in the Old Testament and the Apostles in the New Testament were all of Israeli descent. Israel shared these men with the world.

The Christ: In His humanity, Jesus was a Jewish man. This was Israel's greatest gift to the world.

These unique gifts to the world are Israel's glory and honour. Just as Israel has glory and honour unique to itself, so has every nation, including yours.

Emergence of the Glory and Honour of Israel and World Nations

Satan, through the Pharaoh, a political leader, was restraining Israel's glory and honour from manifesting. That happens to nations governed by ungodly men and women when political and other leaders hold the nation in bondage.

But just as God reserved Moses, Aaron and Miriam for the leadership of Israel, so He is reserving leaders in the nations of the world to take these nations from bondage into their God-given destinies. Canada, Germany, Costa Rica, Haiti, Indonesia, Australia, Nigeria, Bulgaria – these and all other nations, possess God-given glory and honour. You may be ashamed of your nation, or of your leaders, but righteous leadership can uncover and recover your nation's glory and honour.

It is time to contend for the emergence of the greatness of every nation.
It is time.

CHAPTER 3

INFLUENCING THE DESTINIES OF NATIONS

Leaders are influencers. We live in a world that has been created by leaders. Human society, today, is a product of the ideas that passionate visionaries brought from concept to reality. This task of influencing the destinies of nations has been neglected by the church but I see a new day rising, when the light of the revelation of this truth shall activate the leadership spirit in the church, and release a heavenly movement of the 12 types of leaders that shape the destinies of nations.

For too long, large portions of the church have not maximized their callings. This is because many view only the assignment of the Apostle, Prophet, Pastor, Teacher, Evangelist, Deacon and perhaps the Businessman as a calling from God. The rest just go through their daily lives and go to church and pay their tithes and offerings and receive revelation to go through another week of work. This is not the divine pattern. For when you look through the pages of scriptures the callings of men and women were diverse.

The first man, Adam, had a horticultural calling – he was anointed to cultivate a garden --while his wife, Eve, the first woman on earth was anointed to be his helpmate. Unfortunately, instead of giving him fruit from the tree of life, she gave him fruit from the tree of the knowledge of good and evil. Abel looked after cattle and is listed among the elders of faith in Hebrews 11. Noah built a boat. Abraham reared cattle. David and Solomon were Political leaders. Esther was also a Political influencer. These people shaped the destiny of the known world at that time by using the gifts God had given them, in the spheres in which God had called them.

There are 12 spheres of leadership that were revealed to me in a Prophetic dream. They are Spiritual, Philosophic, Political, Military and Law Enforcement, Entrepreneurial, Educational, Family, Judicial, Social Care, Organizational, Media, and Arts & Entertainment. Each sphere influences the destinies of nations in a different way.

Satan understands this and continually positions leaders in all 12 spheres. The church has intentionally raised up leaders in the Spiritual sphere and is now learning about raising up leaders in the Entrepreneurial sphere. However, there are ten other spheres that have been neglected. And we falsely assume that Spiritual leadership alone is able to totally transform the wrong trajectory that a nation is moving toward.

It was revealed in a study of the U.S.A that the arrowhead of Satan's assault on that nation in this season has been through Judicial leaders. He empowered and positioned a critical mass of Judicial leaders who began to militantly legislate lawlessness from the bench, and in the process stripped away vestiges of American Christian values. It was Judicial leadership that legalized abortion, took prayer out of the schools and legalized same-sex marriages. All of our frustrations cannot bring about all that God wants to do in the sphere of American Judicial Leadership, if a critical mass of men and women who fear God and are passionate about legislating and enforcing biblically-based laws are not raised up.

The influence that Spiritual, Entrepreneurial, Military and Political Leadership have on an independent judicial system is not enough to stem the advance of evil.

In California, there are examples of Judicial leaders militantly enforcing laws that were against the democratic wishes and desires of the people concerning same-sex marriages. In nations and communities around the world, there is a combination of drug dealers who are Entrepreneurial leaders, combined with armed gangs and paramilitary groups like the FARC of Colombia who are Military Leaders, creating devastation in nations.

It is time for the 12 types of leaders who go to church every day to rise up, take their role in and influence society!

DEFINITIONS OF THE 12 TYPES OF LEADERSHIP

Spiritual Leadership
Spiritual leadership is the ability to empower, guard and influence people and nations through spiritual authority to discover, live and fulfill the plan and destiny of a sovereign God for them.

Thought Leadership
Philosophic leadership is generational impacting leadership that creates the philosophies that nations use to think, act and organize their affairs.

Political Leadership
Political leadership is the art and science of igniting the passion, deploying the skills and organizing the resources of a people to accomplish a national vision.

Military and Law Enforcement Leadership
Military and Law Enforcement leadership is empowering leadership, that mobilizes people to advance or defend those strategic interests and laws of a people group through the threat or use of lethal force.

Entrepreneurial Leadership
Entrepreneurial leadership creates influence through the income stream it produces, by selling goods and services that meet the needs of people.

Educational Leadership
Educational leadership develops the potential of multitudes through the teaching of knowledge, ideology and skills.

Family Leadership
Family leadership provides vision, guidance, development and resources for the growth and well-being of the immediate and extended family.

Judicial Leadership
Judicial leadership influences nations by creating, interpreting, advocating and enforcing the laws that govern the life of a nation.

Social Care Leadership
Social Care leadership influences nations by creating and operating social enterprises and services that meet the practical needs of a society.

Organizational Leadership

Organizational leadership influences nations by leading the organization of human resources, financial resources and material resources to execute clearly defined missions and goals.

Media Leadership

Media leadership influences nations by selecting, amplifying and distributing the stories, ideas and events that create the information that most people use to make decisions.

Arts and Entertainment Leadership

Arts and Entertainment leadership influences nations by creating the artistic products, entertainment, music and sporting activities that nations celebrate.

UNDERSTANDING LIGHT AND SALT ASSIGNMENTS

In Matthew 5:13-16, Jesus teaches that the Church is the salt of the earth and the light of the world. The Holy Spirit showed me that these twelve assignments can be divided into assignments of light and assignments of salt. Let me explain. Light is overt and it is in your face; it is prominent, it cannot be missed and it stands out in any environment.

So there are those who have been given assignments that are pronounced and prominent in their representation of the Kingdom of God. These assignments of light, fall under the spheres of Spiritual, Thought, Political, Military and Law Enforcement, Entrepreneurial and Educational leadership.

Salt is different. When salt is applied to soup or to meat, it becomes invisible to the naked eye but its impact and its effect is tremendous. The effect of salt is transformational, yet it is not as prominent in its appearance as light. So there are those who have salt assignments. Their effect on society will be tremendous yet they are largely unnoticed to the casual observer.

These salt assignments fall under the spheres of Family, Judicial, Social Care, Organizational, Media and Arts & Entertainment leadership.

Let us now study each sphere of leadership and some of the biblical, historical and contemporary figures that have shaped them.

The12 Spheres of Leadership

CHAPTER FOUR

THE DYNAMICS OF SPIRITUAL LEADERSHIP

Spiritual leadership is the ability to empower, guard and influence people and nations through spiritual authority to discover, live and fulfill the plan and destiny of a sovereign God for them.

Man is a spirit. He has a soul and he lives in a body. He is not a physical being seeking a spiritual experience but a spiritual being having a temporal, physical experience. The world that we know was made by God who is a spirit and lives in the world of the spirit called the heavens.

Jesus said to the woman at the well, 'God is a spirit and they that worship Him must worship Him in spirit and in truth' (John 4:24). This world of matter that we live in came out of the world of the spirit. It is therefore subject to the world of the spirit and its destiny is determined by the forces that rule the world of the spirit.

Spiritual leadership brings the agenda of the world of the spirit into the reality of the temporal material world. God and his arch enemy Satan are both spirits and they utilize spiritual leaders to bring to pass their agendas on the earth. These agendas always have to do with destiny. The word destiny simply means a pre-determined end.

Our precious heavenly Father has a destiny for nations, churches, organizations, families and individuals—and finds great pleasure when we are walking in the fullness of this destiny which is the best version of ourselves. Satan also has a destiny for nations, churches, organizations, families and individuals and he works through his agents on the earth to bring that destiny to pass.

Spiritual leadership is destiny releasing leadership. It is the destiny of an apple seed to become an apple tree producing apples. It is the destiny of a mango seed to become a mango tree producing mangoes. It is the destiny of a pear seed to become a pear tree producing pears.

"Then sending the crowds away, Jesus went into the house. And His disciples came to Him, saying; explain to us the parable of the darnel of the field. He answered and said to them, He who sows the good seed is the Son of Man; the field is the world; the good seed are the sons of the kingdom; but the darnel are the sons of the evil one. The enemy who sowed them is the Devil; the harvest is the end of the world; and the reapers are the angels. Therefore, as the darnel are gathered and burned in the fire, so it shall be in the end of this world. The Son of Man shall send out His angels, and they shall gather out of His kingdom all things that offend, and those who do iniquity, and shall cast them into a furnace of fire. There shall be wailing and gnashing of teeth. Then the righteous shall shine out like the sun in the kingdom of their Father. He, who has ears to hear, let him hear (Matthew 13:36-43)."

Jesus in explaining the mystery of the kingdom of God hidden in the parable of the wheat and tares reveals striking insights:

1. People are seed and the good seed are the children of the kingdom of God while the bad seed are the children of the wicked one.
2. Satan follows God's pattern and sows people seed into the world.

Every seed does not look like its destiny. If you purchase lettuce seeds, they do not look like the lettuce that is inside the seed. However, in order to bring forth the lettuce that the seed is pregnant with, the seed has to be put into good soil, cultivated, watered and then harvested.

The children of the kingdom in their seed stage never look or behave like their destiny. They require spiritual leaders who will provide the good soil of God's Word and His anointing for them to become planted in. They then require care, prayer and water to be cultivated to produce the destiny fruit that is within them.

God's Spiritual leaders provide water to cultivate the destinies in nations, cities, towns, churches, organizations, families, and people by modeling, preaching, teaching, praying, counseling, and practical service. The reason why it takes spiritual leadership to do this is simply because the destiny of a tomato seed is invisible to the naked eye and it takes someone who sees in the invisible what that tomato seed can become to take the time to plant, cultivate, water, and harvest it.

In the same way, the divine destiny of nations, churches, organizations, families, and individuals is invisible to the naked eye but very real in the realm of the spirit, which is the realm of the invisible. Spiritual leaders are supposed to see the invisible destiny in a person or entity and use their spiritual authority and gifts to cultivate the full manifestation of its destiny. It is spiritual because destiny is invisible to the naked eye. This is why Jesus used agricultural parables to describe many of the aspects of the kingdom of heaven. Farmers operate in the invisible when they plant seed in the ground and take steps to release the pre-destined fruit in the seed.

Spiritual leaders are farmers. Jesus said the sower sows the Word inferring that God's Word in itself is seed. God's Word operates like a seed and people also operate like a seed. Spiritual leadership is however not limited to just the Kingdom of God but Satan employs and utilizes his own spiritual leaders with great effectiveness.

The children of the wicked one who are unsaved do not have the seed of the divine nature on the inside of them. They have the seed of the sin nature on the inside of them and Satan uses his spiritual leaders to create the soil and provides cultivation for the full manifestation of sin in people. He calls forth for the destiny of sin in people which is hell on earth and eternity. Demonic spiritual leaders do the same thing that spiritual leaders of God's kingdom do:

- They pray to Satan for the release of demonic spirits to bring the satanic agenda, which is to steal, kill and destroy on the earth (John 10:10). We call this witchcraft, Voodoo, Juju and sorcery.
- They teach and preach doctrines of demons (1 Tim. 4:1).
- They provide demonic inspired counseling through the new age and psychics.
- They fast and sacrifice to gain greater spiritual power.
- They praise and worship Satan as their god through satanically inspired music from popular celebrities.
- They work with singers and musicians to popularize the doctrines of demons. We call these singers pop stars.
- They spread their message through every form of mass communication.

- They inspire people to fund the agenda of Satan by promoting enchanted articles, books and music that millions of people buy.

When Satan manifests himself in the earth realm during the period of time call 'The Great Tribulation,' as revealed in the Book of Revelation chapter 13 —we see that his two major instruments are the Anti-Christ who is a political leader and the False Prophet who is a Spiritual leader.

Jesus in Matthew Chapter 24 spoke about false prophets and false Christs arising in the last days. These are Spiritual leaders empowered by hell to deceive the masses.

Demonic Spiritual leaders come in all shapes and sizes with varying levels of influence. Some have great influence while others have trans-generational influence and create religions that compete against Christianity. Some have lesser influence and they influence the people in their world to worship the demonic, and to follow the doctrines of demons that cultivate the worst in them. These demonic Spiritual leaders have influenced nations from the beginning of time and lead people to hell.

If you are called to be a Spiritual leader, then your spiritual gift would be listed in one of these three bible lists:

1. Ephesians 4:11 -13

Apostles
Those sent by God to break new ground for the kingdom of God and establish heavenly movements in the earth.

Prophets
Those gifted to be the mouthpiece of a specific agenda of God to a people group.

Evangelists
Those gifted to throw the net of the Gospel and bring in a harvest of unsaved people into the kingdom of God and stir up the saints.

Pastors
Those gifted to feed, care and guide a specific flock of God's people into their destiny.

Teachers
Those that are gifted to bring freedom to God's people through the illumination of truth.

2. Romans 12:6 -8

Ministry of Prophesy
Those gifted to speak by sudden inspiration of the moment to the church for comfort, exhortation and edification.

The Gift of Service
Those anointed to provide practical services to individuals such as administration, hospitality, etc., that advance the agenda of God.

The Gift of Exhortation
Those anointed to motivate and proclaim truths to people that ignite them for action.

The Gift of Giving
Those anointed to acquire significant financial and material resources,

and utilize them to fund the fulfillment of specific God-given agendas that are to be carried out by churches and ministries.

The Gift of Organizational Leadership
This is a gift of those who are called to manage human, material and financial resources in the church to accomplish a predefined agenda of God.

Mercy Gift
Those who are anointed to provide practical help to the poor and afflicted in society.

3. 1 Corinthians 12

Apostles, Prophets and Teachers as listed above.

Miracle Ministry
Those that have a ministry of continual access to the divine power of God, and releasing it in real time to advance the agenda of God and undo the works of darkness among people.

Healing Ministry
Those anointed by God to access the healing anointing of Jesus Christ and administer it to destroy sicknesses, diseases and infirmities in the lives of people.

Helps Ministry
Those anointed to help the spread and impact of the message, anointing and grace of five-fold ministry leaders by providing spiritual and organizational support that excludes preaching and teaching. E.g., Intercessory Prayer ministry, Music ministry and Media ministry.

Governments (Same as Organizational Leadership Gift in Romans 12)

Diversities of Tongues
Those anointed to use the agency of speaking in unknown tongues and the resulting interpretation to communicate messages to God's people that provide comfort, edification and exhortation.

Spiritual leaders have always shaped the destinies of villages, towns, cities and nations. In the scriptures, two of the greatest examples of this can be found in the lives of Elijah, a senior prophet of God who raised up a school of prophets. Then Jezebel, a prophetess of Satan who raised up an army of the prophets of Baal.

ELIJAH: A PROPHET THAT PRESERVED THE DESTINY OF ISRAEL

The prophet Elijah was called into the ministry during one of the most dangerous times in the history of Israel. Satan, through strategy, had gained a vice like grip on the destiny of the nation and was taking it in the direction of witchcraft and the worship of demons. The marriage of Ahab to Jezebel had formed a powerful alliance for evil that was threatening to derail God's plans for the nation.

It is against this backdrop of evil, that the Spirit of God introduces the prophet Elijah. He was an unusual prophet as he was a Signs and Wonders prophet and his mandate was not just to declare the times and seasons of God—but to change the times and seasons on earth to reflect God's agenda, which he did.

One day he walked into the king's palace and gave a short prophetic word that released the judgment of drought on the nation (1 Kings 17:1). The next time he appeared to the king he announced to him that the Lord will send rain again upon the nation. He then called for all the 450 prophets of Baal and the 400 prophets of the groves which ate at Jezebel's table to a confrontation on top of Mount Carmel.

In the true way of a prophet that carries a demonstration of the spirit in signs and wonders he challenged the prophet of Baal and the groves to a supernatural contest. He asked them to call fire to come down from heaven on a sacrifice. The prophets of Baal attempt to do that but did not succeed. Elijah stepped up and prayed a one sentence prayer and the scripture says in 1 Kings 18:38 that the fire of the Lord fell and consumed the burnt sacrifice, the wood, the stone, the dust and the water.

When the people of Israel saw this, they fell on their faces and declared that the Lord is God. Elijah then issued a command and told the people who witnessed this demonstration of God's power to take the Prophets of Baal and let none escape. Elijah then went and slew all 400 of them. Afterwards he announced to King Ahab that the abundance of rain would now come after the slaying and destruction of the prophetic institution that his wife Jezebel had built.

JEZEBEL: A SENIOR PROPHETESS OF SATAN

Jezebel, Ahab's wife also had a similar agenda which she had executed before Elijah the prophet came on the scene. Inspired by Satan, she had slain the Prophets of the Lord but Obadiah, a man who feared God, had succeeded in hiding a group of prophets in a cave when Jezebel attempted to wipe out the Prophetic word of the Lord to Israel. (For it was *so,* when Jezebel cut off the prophets of the

LORD, that Obadiah took a hundred prophets, and hid them by fifty in a cave, and fed them with bread and water.1Kings 18:4)

When Jezebel heard that Elijah the Prophet of the Lord had outdone her, she sent a message that she will ensure that Elijah dies the same death that her prophets had suffered at his hand. It was a clash of spiritual leaders; one for the kingdom of God and one for the kingdom of darkness. This battle is played out day in and day out in the nations of the world.

We then see Elijah the prophet who is wounded by the demonically inspired words of Jezebel run in fear of his life. In his mind the forces of darkness operating in the nation of Israel suddenly became too much for him. The Lord sends His angels to strengthen him and he is instructed to go and meet with the Lord at Horeb, the mount of God. At this mountain, he receives divine instructions that would release the agenda of God in the nation and defeat the satanic agenda entrusted to Jezebel.

And it was so, when Elijah heard it, that he wrapped his face in his mantle, and went out, and stood in the entering in of the cave. And, behold, there came a voice unto him, and said, "What doest thou here, Elijah?" And he said, "I have been very jealous for the LORD God of hosts: because the children of Israel have forsaken thy covenant, thrown down thine altars, and slain thy prophets with the sword; and I, even I only, am left; and they seek my life, to take it away."
And the LORD said unto him, "Go, return on thy way to the wilderness of Damascus: and when thou comest, anoint Hazael to be king over Syria: And Jehu the son of Nimshi shalt thou anoint to be king over Israel: and Elisha the son of Shaphat of Abelmeholah shalt thou anoint to be prophet in thy room. And it shall come to pass, that him that escapeth the sword of Hazael shall Jehu slay: and him that

escapeth from the sword of Jehu shall Elisha slay (1Kings 19:13-17)."

Jehu eventually slayed Jezebel and Elisha succeeded Elijah with a double of the anointing and power that Elijah had, and the destiny of Israel was preserved.

In this day and time when witches, warlocks, new agers and various forms of occult are growing in influence, ministers in the order of Elijah are being released to change the trajectory of nations.

If you have been called to be a spiritual leader, there isn't a better time than now to shine by advancing the agenda of God and defeating the agenda of the devil in the territory to which you are assigned.

JOHN WESLEY: A REFORMER FROM HEAVEN

When we study Church history, one of the men that have had an Elijah- like impact on his nation was John Wesley who lived in the 1700s. He lived in a time when the nation of Great Britain was in the grip of all types of vices and he, by the supernatural enablement entrusted to him, rode 25000 miles by horse back to preach the gospel – a distance comparable to circling the globe ten times.

He preached more than 40,000 sermons and published more than 5000 pamphlets and books of all kinds. His life can be captured in this saying, "I looked upon all the world as my parish; thus far I mean, that, in whatsoever part of it I am, I judge it meet, right, and my duty to declare unto all that are willing to hear, the glad tidings of salvation."

John brought the challenge of living for Christ to the English Church that was in dire need of revival. He and his brother

Charles' endeavors were not only limited to England but to continental Europe and America. He became the father of the Methodist Church and paved the way for successive moves of God.

His ministry was not limited to preaching the gospel in large open air meetings, but he also planted churches which kept the fruit of his ministry and preserved it for successive generations.

Today most nations in the western world have Methodist churches due to his efforts. He was a trans-generational world changer.

Whilst you may not have John Wesley's gifting you can certainly follow his passion, focus and perseverance in fulfilling his heavenly mandate. Arise and change your world.

ANTON LE VAY: A GROUND BREAKER FOR SATAN

Satan, not wanting to be undone, has his own apostles that plant churches and in Anton LaVay we saw an ambassador of Satan to a generation. He was born on April 11, 1930 and lived until October 29, 1997, and was the founder of the church of Satan as well as a writer, occultist and musician. He was the author of the Satanic bible and founder of Laveyan Satanism, a sensitized system of doctrines of demons on human nature and the insights of demonically inspired philosophers who advocated materialism and individualism.

Anton began his mission as a Satanic ambassador by presenting Friday night lectures on the occult and rituals, and in April 1966 he declared the founding of the church of Satan and proclaimed 1966 as the year Anno Satananas- The first year as the age of Satan. He wrote many essays and books such as The *Satanic Witch* and *Satanic Rituals* and laid the foundation for the rise of Satanism among western civilization.

He was an in your face agent of the kingdom of darkness. There are similar agents in your nation today and the only reason why they prevail is because the agents of the light of the glorious gospel of Jesus Christ have not manifested yet.

The Charge

If you are called to Spiritual leadership, do not fear the work of Satan. Darkness only prospers in the absence of light. Arise in your calling and your gifting and let the light of God shine through you and it would be unto you "and the light shineth in darkness and the darkness comprehended it not (John 1:4-5)."

End Notes

1. Robert Southey, *The Life of Wesley and the Rise and Progress of Methodism* (London: Frederick Warne and Company Ltd., n.d., ca. 1820), 11

2. Anton LeVay Wikipedia

CHAPTER FIVE

THE DYNAMICS OF PHILOSOPHIC LEADERSHIP

Philosophic leadership is generational impacting leadership that creates the philosophies that nations use to think, act and organize their affairs.

The impact of philosophic leadership is not realized by much of the world's population, yet this small group of leaders has created the thought systems, philosophies and ideologies billions of people use to think and make decisions.

This fact was burnt into my heart one day while teaching an ethics and citizenship class to students at a national college. Much of the curriculum involved teaching the major philosophies that had shaped the thinking of western civilization and I wanted to empower my students to question the ideas and world views that they had accepted as normal.

I presented a twenty- five-year strategic plan of the government of Barbados and I asked my students to get a copy each—I then divided the class into two groups and asked them to study the plan and tell me the school of philosophical thought that produced the plan.

When they presented the assignments, one group of students stated that eighty-five percent of the Strategic Plan for the nation, written by the government was shaped and molded in the school of Pluto, one of Greece's foremost philosophers. The other fifteen percent of the plan was shaped in the school of Aristotle, another Greek philosopher.

These men had been dead for hundreds of years, yet their ideas and thoughts were shaping the thinking, policies, plans and actions of a small Caribbean country thousands of miles from Greece. Men die but thoughts and ideas do not die. Men cannot rule for thousands of years but their thoughts and ideas can rule for thousands of years.

Thought leaders create the ideas and philosophies that rule the world. When they are holy and godly they discover and promote ideologies and philosophies of heavenly origin. These ideas and philosophies release life, joy, peace, blessing and progress on the earth.

When these thought leaders receive their inspiration from demons they create ideas, philosophies and worldviews that strengthen the work of the kingdom of darkness on the earth.

Your nation is ruled by ideas. They could be democratic, socialist, totalitarian, hedonistic, pragmatic, liberal or conservative ideas. These ideas cover every spectrum of life.

To understand this, let's go deeper. The Word of God reveals two primary things. It reveals the person of God and the principles of God. You can know the person of God and not be acquainted with the principles of God. When God spoke to Moses who was a spiritual and philosophic leader, He not only revealed His person but He also revealed His thoughts on issues like manslaughter, diet, marriage and national life. He gave him a code of ethics called the Ten Commandments.

It is interesting to know that the Satanic bible written by Anton LaVay also has commandments that reveal the ideologies of Satan. The first commandment of the Satanic bible states, "If it feels good do it". This may not sound evil to the casual observer, however, if the ruler of your nation sets aside a day for citizens to do what they feel like with no consequences, you would most likely skip town as it will unleash an outpouring of evil in your nation.

Demonic philosophies are called the doctrine of demons and Satan raises up philosophic leaders to advance his agenda and create ideal conditions for demons to do their dirty work of stealing, killing and destroying. If you have within you the gifting of a philosophic leader, you can be used to bring the logic, principles and philosophies of God in a field of human endeavor.

Philosophic leaders sometimes create thought incubators called think tanks that create ideologies that govern the decisions that nations make. The world is in need of more biblically based think tanks that cover the key spheres of national life.

Philosophic leaders tend to specialize in particular areas. Some focus on morality, some on foreign policy, some on economics, some on family, some on education, some on science and technology and the list goes on. I am gifted to be a philosophic leader and my focus is economic dignity and national greatness.

In the school of philosophic leadership Moses is a giant. God gave him The Ten Commandments, which became the moral philosophical code of conduct for nations founded on Judo-Christian values.

And God spoke all these words, saying:

"I am the LORD your God, who brought you out of the land of Egypt, out of the house of bondage. "You shall have no other gods before Me "You shall not make for yourself a carved image—any likeness of anything that is in heaven above, or that is in the earth beneath, or that is in the water under the earth; you shall not bow down to them nor serve them.

For I, the LORD your God, am a jealous God, visiting the iniquity of the fathers upon the children to the third and fourth generations of those who hate Me, but showing mercy to thousands, to those who love Me and keep My commandments. "You shall not take the name of the LORD your God in vain, for the LORD will not hold him guiltless who takes His name in vain.

"Remember the Sabbath day, to keep it holy. Six days you shall labor and do all your work, but the seventh day is the Sabbath of the LORD your God. In it you shall do no work: you, nor your son, nor your daughter, nor your male servant, nor your female servant, nor your cattle, nor your stranger who is within your gates. For in six days the LORD made the heavens and the earth, the sea, and all that is in them, and rested the seventh day. Therefore, the LORD blessed the Sabbath day and hallowed it. "Honor your father and your mother, that your days may be long upon the land which the LORD your God is giving you.

"You shall not murder.
"You shall not commit adultery.
"You shall not steal.
"You shall not bear false witness against your neighbor.
"You shall not covet your neighbor's house; you shall not covet your neighbor's wife, nor his male servant, nor his female servant, nor

his ox, nor his donkey, nor anything that is your neighbor's (Exodus 20:1-17**).***"*

This divine ideology is the foundation of the legal system in western civilization. It has given birth to the laws that govern murder, theft and divorce on the grounds of adultery. It has affected the work week in most nations. There are still biblical ideologies that our world today needs to become enlightened by and God is still sending His philosophic leaders to this generation.

EPICUREAN PHILOSOPHERS

"Now while Paul waited for them at Athens, his spirit was provoked within him when he saw that the city was given over to idols. Therefore, he reasoned in the synagogue with the Jews and with the Gentile worshippers, and in the marketplace daily with those who happened to be there. Then certain Epicurean and Stoic philosophers encountered him. And some said, "What does this babbler want to say?" Others said, "He seems to be a proclaimer of foreign gods," because he preached to them Jesus and the resurrection. And they took him and brought him to the Areopagus, saying, "May we know what this new doctrine is of which you speak? For you are bringing some strange things to our ears. Therefore, we want to know what these things mean." For all the Athenians and the foreigners who were there spent their time in nothing else but either to tell or to hear some new thing (Acts 17: 16-21)."

We can see from the scriptures that in the Bible times, as it is today, there was a clash of ideologies.

John Hayward in his book the *Nook of Religions* states

that:

"The disciples of Epicurus, who flourished about A. M.3700. This sect maintained that the world was formed not by God, nor with any design, but by the fortuitous concourse of atoms. They denied that God governs the world, or in the least condescends to interfere with creatures below; they denied the immortality of the soul, and the existence of angels; they maintained that happiness consisted in pleasure; but some of them placed this pleasure in the tranquility and joy of the mind, arising from the practice of moral virtue, and which is thought by some to have been the true principle of Epicurus: others understood him in the gross sense, and placed all their happiness in corporeal pleasure.

When Paul was at Athens, he had conferences with the Epicurean philosophers. The word *Epicurean* is used at present for an indolent, effeminate, and voluptuous person, who only consults his private and particular pleasure."

The ideologies of demons clashed with the ideologies of God for dominance among people in the nations.

Two examples of philosophic leaders whose ideologies are affecting the world are John Maxwell and Charles F. Porter:

JOHN MAXWELL: A PHILOSOPHIC LEADER AND AUTHORITY ON LEADERSHIP.

Dr. John Maxwell has written over 70 books, sold over 20 million books and has become the world's leading authority on leadership,

John Maxwell's organizations have trained more than five million leaders worldwide. He is the founder of The John Maxwell Co., INJOY Stewardship Services and EQUIP, an international leadership development organization working to help leaders. EQUIP is involved with leaders from more than 80 nations. Its mission is "to see effective Christian leaders fulfill the Great Commission in every nation".

Every year Maxwell speaks to Fortune 500 companies, international government leaders, and organizations as diverse as the United States Military Academy at West Point and the National Football League. He is a *New York Times*, *Wall Street Journal*, and *Business Week* best-selling author. His biblical philosophy of leadership has had a transformative effect on this generation.

One of the great privileges of my life is to serve as a global partner with his organization Equip. It has helped me to grow as a leader and learn the art of influencing people with biblical leadership wisdom.

CHARLES F. POTTER: A HUMANISTIC PHILOSOPHIC LEADER THAT IGNITED THE RIPPLE EFFECT OF GODLESSNESS IN WESTERN EDUCATION.

In the 1930's Charles F. Potter, Liberal Education Philosopher, along with other Philosophic Leaders, developed *a new set of doctrines called the Humanist Manifesto* which denies the existence of a supernatural being.

"Humanism is not the abolition of religion, but the beginning of real religion. By freeing religion of supernaturalism, it will release tremendous reserves of hitherto thwarted power. Man has waited too long for God to do what man ought to do himself and is fully capable of doing." It was to be, he said, "a religion of common

sense; and the chief end of man is to improve himself, both as an individual and as a race."

Through his direct efforts humanism has become the doctrine of liberal arts universities the world over. His philosophy can be summed in this statement:

"Education is the most powerful ally of Humanism, and every public school is a school of Humanism. What can the theistic Sunday School, meeting for an hour once a week, and teaching only a fraction of the children, do to stem the tide of a five-day program of humanistic teaching?"

The Charge
If you are called to the sphere of Philosophic leadership understand that the philosophies of God are the foundation of the greatness of nations. God has a philosophy on every aspect of your nation's life and he reveals it to his vessels who share it with humanity. At no other time in history has the battle over ideology been so fierce as anti-Christ Philosophic leaders seek to transform nations with the doctrines of demons. So stand up in your area of specialization and be a voice of God thoughts to nations.

End Notes
1. EPICUREANS. The Book of Religions; John Hayward

2. Injoy.com

3. *Charles F. Potter, Humanism: A New Religion (1930).*

CHAPTER 6

THE DYNAMICS OF POLITICAL LEADERSHIP

Political Leadership is the art and science of igniting the passion, deploying the skills and organizing the resources of a people to accomplish a national vision.

Politics is **the art or science of governing a country's internal and external relations.** True political visionaries are a rare breed. They are shapers of the destinies of nations through politics. Their focus is three-fold:

1. **Governance** utilizes government to govern and impact the lives of citizens.
2. **Campaigning** aims at getting into and staying in political office.
3. **Policy Creation** focuses on creating polices that advance and defends the nation's strategic interests.

There are two types of political visionaries:

Habitual leaders - people who have a natural inclination to lead in almost any circumstance.

Situational leaders - people whose leadership genius only emerges when they find themselves by design or accident in a situation that matches their passion, gifting, intelligence and skill sets.

In order to establish a platform of understanding, the words '*vision*', and '*political visionary*' will be defined as follows:

A vision is a clear mental portrait of a preferred future.

A political visionary is a person who possesses both a clear, compelling mental portrait of the potential of a town, city or nation, and the innate potential to take that vision from concept to reality.

A person who has a vision for the potential of the city but does not have innate potential to bring it to pass is a *political dreamer*. There are many political dreamers in office. The threshold of the ability of political visionaries is ordered in ranks.

It comes in measures that determine a visionary's capacity to lead. Some do not have the gifting to aspire beyond a certain level. The threshold of their ability may only be for governing a village. For others, it may be for a town, a city, a region, or a nation.

Thresholds of ability in leaders vary according to their gifting and leadership growth. Great political visionaries may be gifted for the roles of mayors, ministers of parliament, governors, leaders within political parties and presidents.

In a study of the Old Testament, I discovered that some of God's most valuable leaders were Political Leaders. They were called Kings. David was a Political leader who became the greatest King of Israel. Joseph was the Prime Minister of Egypt anointed to fill a political office. Esther used her political office as the queen to save the Jews from extinction. Why is the office of the Political Leader so important?

Political leaders determine the type of governance under which a nation creates its moral, social, economic and national defense climate.

Political leaders of every rank bring four defining features with them into political office:

1. **Political ideology** – how they think a nation should be governed with respect to its internal and external relations.
2. **Political agenda** – the program they want to implement using the power of their political office.
3. **Motive** – the reason they want to be in political leadership.
4. **Leadership competence** – their ability to marshal human, financial and material resources to accomplish a vision.

Based on these four defining features, let's compare the Scriptural political leadership styles of David the King of Israel and the ruler of Tyre.

KING OF TYRE: A BRILLIANT POLITICAL BEAST

"The Word of Jehovah came again to me, saying, Son of man, say to the ruler of Tyre. So says the Lord Jehovah: Because your heart is lifted up, and you have said, I am a god, I sit in the seat of God, in the midst of the seas; yet you are a man and not God, though you set your heart as the heart of gods; Behold, you are wiser than Daniel; all secret things are not hidden from you! With your wisdom and with your understanding you have made riches for yourselves, and have worked gold and silver into your treasuries.

By your great wisdom and by your trade you have multiplied your riches, and your heart is lifted up because of your riches. Therefore, so says the Lord Jehovah: Because you have set your heart as the heart of gods, behold, therefore I will bring awesome strangers of the nations. And they shall draw their swords against the beauty of your wisdom, and they shall defile your brightness.

They shall bring you down to the Pit, and you shall die the deaths of those slain in the heart of the seas. Will you yet say before him who kills you, I am of the gods? But you are a man, and not God, in the hand of him who kills you. You shall die the deaths of the uncircumcised by the hand of strangers. For I have spoken, says the Lord Jehovah.

And the Word of Jehovah came to me, saying, Son of man, lift up a lament over the king of Tyre, and say to him, So says the Lord Jehovah: You seal the measure, full of wisdom and perfect in beauty. You have been in Eden the garden of God; every precious stone was your covering, the ruby, topaz, and the diamond, the beryl, the onyx, and the jasper, the sapphire, the turquoise, and the emerald, and gold.

The workmanship of your tambourines and of your flutes was prepared in you in the day that you were created. You were the anointed cherub that covers, and I had put you in the holy height of God where you were; you have walked up and down in the midst of the stones of fire. You were perfect in your ways from the day that you were created, until iniquity was found in you.

By the multitude of your goods they have filled your midst with violence, and you have sinned. So I cast you profaned from the height of God, and I destroy you, O covering cherub, from among the stones of fire. Your heart was lifted up because of your beauty; you have spoiled your wisdom because of your bright- ness. I will cast you to the ground; I will put you before kings, that they may behold you.

By the host of your iniquities, by the iniquity of your trade, you have profaned your holy places; so I brought a fire from your midst; it shall devour you, and I will give you for ashes on the earth, before the eyes of all who see you. All who know you among the peoples shall be astonished at you; you shall be terrors, and you will not be forever (Ezekiel 28:1-19)."

DAVID: A POLITICAL LEADER AFTER GOD'S HEART

"Now these be the last words of David. David, the son of Jesse said, and the man who was raised up on high, the anointed of the God of Jacob, and the sweet psalmist of Israel, said, The Spirit of the LORD spake by me, and his word was in my tongue. The God of Israel said, the Rock of Israel spake to me, He that ruleth over men must be just, ruling in the fear of God. And he shall be as the light of the morning, when the sun riseth, even a morning without clouds; as the tender grass springing out of the earth by clear shining after rain" (2 Samuel 23:1-4)."

Political ideology: The Political ideology of the ruler of Tyre was to govern for the purpose of increasing personal power and amassing personal riches and wealth. The Political Ideology of David was to govern in such a way that God could release His purposes through the nation.

Political agenda: The Political agenda of the ruler of Tyre was to be a god. The Political Agenda of David was to establish the dominion of Israel and the supremacy of Jehovah, the God of Israel.

Personal motivation: The motive of the ruler of Tyre was to be worshipped. The motive of David was to serve Israel by the will of God.

Leadership competence: The political ruler of Tyre led with distinct political brilliance given to him by the devil and was only defeated by an Act of God. Whilst David, led by the supremacy of divine wisdom, was supported by God.

Let's now look at a transformational political leader from history

ERROL BARROW: A POLITICAL DELIVERER

Acclaimed as the father of Barbados' independence, Errol Walton Barrow was born in the Parish of St. Lucy on January 21, 1920. A founding member of the Democratic Labour Party, Barrow swept to power as Premier in 1961 and held that position until 1966. He became Barbados' first Prime Minister when his party won the elections in 1966-1976 and again in 1985-1987, and took the island into independence from Britain.

Among his many great accomplishments, the visionary course he set for Barbados and the national identity he infused into the people stands out. It is said he found a collection of villages and left it a proud country.

Former Prime Minister Owen Arthur of Barbados in a 2007 speech honoring the legacy of Errol Barrow, eloquently speaks about his visionary legacy in these words:

"Mr. Barrow was first and foremost driven by a passion to make the Barbadian people great, not only insofar as the region was concerned, but also in the family of nations, both developing and developed. He possessed an unwavering dedication to a vision of world-class status for the Caribbean region's most industrious small nation. As early as 1950, he visualized the possibility of Barbados becoming a world class s o c i e t y. Thus, this dedicated nationalist let down his bucket in Barbados in the 1950s, first as a lieutenant to the venerable Sir Grantley Adams, then striking out on his own and creating his own mass-based political force the Democratic Labor Party.

The question may be asked – what distinguished the Right Excellent Errol Barrow from other Barbadian (and Caribbean) leaders of his era? There are five and possibly six areas that can be identified in which Mr. Barrow so acquitted himself as to be regarded by most people as the "Father of Modern Barbados."

Firstly, Mr. Barrow was a crusader on behalf of the common man. His care and concern for our working class was almost legendary. His was a lifelong campaign to eliminate poverty and wretchedness from Barbados. Then there is Barrow the great revolutionary and father of independence. Many thousands of words have been written and spoken of his bold decision in 1965 to press for constitutional independence for this island.

Mr. Barrow correctly gauged the eagerness and enthusiasm of the Barbadian masses for their freedom from Britain's imperial embrace, and led us to that glorious date with destiny on the 30th day of November 1966. Time has not diminished nor dimmed the luster of that wonderful occasion, nor have events conspired to make our recollections of November 1966 bitter ones.

On the contrary, the new nation which he ushered in that year is now standing near the threshold of First World status and is currently pressing for acceptance as a world-class society. Thirdly, we must take note of Errol Barrow, the Visionary Educator – the man who completed the Grantley Adams program of liberating education from the clutches of class and racial prejudices.

We laud and magnify his name whenever our children write the 11-plus Common Entrance Examination each year and whenever they contentedly eat their school meals each school-day. We continue to express our admiration for the man who introduced the pioneering concept of the Barbados Community College in 1968, and we stand in awe when we remember that he single-handedly, introduced university education to Barbados in 1963 with the opening of what was to become the Cave Hill Campus.

Mr. Barrow was a builder and his work observed all around us. There is the Treasury Building, the First National Insurance Building, the Middle Income Housing Developments of the 1960s and the 1970s; the Industrial Estates, the expansion to the Airport and the Seaport and a number of schools, such as, Ellerslie Secondary, Parkinson Secondary and St. Lucy Secondary Schools.

Mr. Barrow's magnanimity and passion for harmony also inspire us with respect and admiration. This is the fifth area of glorious achievement during his term of office, 1961 to 1987 and particularly after 1966, when several voices questioned the wisdom of his decision to take Barbados into Independence alone.

Mr. Barrow assumed the mantle of a statesman and held out the "olive branch" to the former plantation and commercial elites who had ruled Barbados up to the 1940s. To them, he became the harbinger of democracy, progress, harmony and cooperation.

He practiced the politics of inclusiveness long before it became a total force in the 21st century, making whites, Jews, Muslims, Hindus and other ethnic minorities in this society feel comfortable and safe. Simultaneously, he overturned the culture of racial discrimination and secured for all Barbadians their fundamental rights. To all Barbadians he was "the Great Reconciler."

There is a sixth arena in which he shone like a beacon of progressiveness and cooperation – the pertinent sphere of regional integration. It is an important aspect of the traditions of Barbadian leaders, that a significant part of their lifework should be dedicated to the cause of advancing Caribbean unity. No tribute to this National Hero and Caribbean man would be complete, without a generous mention of his valiant efforts to promote cooperation among Britain's former colonies in the Caribbean.

Along with Eric Williams and Vere Bird, he was one of the Founding Fathers of CARIFTA in 1965. With Manley, Williams and Burnham, he was at the founding of CARICOM in 1973. This transformational political leader laid the foundation and set the course for significant development in Barbados and its present ranking of 31 on the United Nations Development Program Human Index."

The Holy Spirit spoke these words upon me, "*Unless a critical mass of righteous men and women are in the political system, the atmosphere of the nation will favor the work of the devil rather than the work of God and the destiny of the nation will be endangered."*

But you may ask, would God raise a critical mass of righteous men and women into office? He is well able, if the Church stops persecuting God's sons and daughters called to be political influencers. To be brutally frank, a Church that folds its hands and does not participate in the political process or persecutes Christians involved in the political process is unconsciously aiding the agenda of the devil in its nation.

When the called are willing and the Church is spiritually intelligent, God will raise up Daniels, Shadrachs, Meshachs and Abednegos who are anointed for politics and will influence their "Babylon," stirring it along the path of God's plan. When the called are willing and the Church is spiritually intelligent, God can raise up Josephs who can deploy the nation's resources to support the agenda of God.

When the called are willing and the Church is spiritually intelligent, God can raise up Esthers who can use their access to the King to preserve the destiny of God's people.

The hour has come for us to stop surrendering the political office to the forces of wickedness. It is time for a new breed of political visionaries to arise out of the body of Christ and bring the righteous agenda of God to bear on the governance of towns, cities, states, provinces and nations.

If you are called to the sphere of political leadership, you can do the same in your nation.

NICOLAE CEAUȘESCU: A POLITICAL LEADER WHO BECAME A TYRANT

Nicolae Ceaușescu was a communist official who was leader of Romania from 1965 until he was overthrown and killed in a revolution in December 1989. A prominent member of the Romanian Communist youth movement during the early 1930s, Ceausescu was imprisoned in 1936 and again in 1940 for his Communist Party activities.

In 1939 he married Elena Petrescu who was a devout Communist. While in prison, Ceausescu became a protégé of his cell mate Gheorghe Gheorghiu-Dej, who would become the Communist leader of Romania beginning in 1952.

Escaping prison in August 1944 shortly before the Soviet occupation of Romania, Ceausescu subsequently served as secretary of the Union of Communist Youth (1944-1945).

After the Communists' full accession to power in Romania in 1947, he first headed the nation's ministry of agriculture (1948-1950), and from 1950-1954 he served as Deputy Minister of the armed forces with the rank of Major General. Under Gheorghiu-Dej, Ceausescu eventually came to occupy the second highest position in the party hierarchy holding important posts in the Politburo and Secretariat.

With the death of Gheorghiu Dej in March 1965, Ceausescu succeeded to the leadership of Romania's Communist Party, first as secretary (General Secretary from July 1965) and with his assumption of the Presidency of the State Council (December 1967), he became Head of State as well. He soon won popular support for his independent, nationalistic political course, which openly challenged the dominance of the Soviet Union over Romania.

In the 1960s Ceausescu virtually ended Romania's active participation in the Warsaw Pact military alliance, and he condemned the invasion of Czechoslovakia by Warsaw Pact and the invasion of Afghanistan by the Soviet Union (1979). Ceausescu was elected to the newly created post of president of Romania in 1974.

While following an independent policy in foreign relations, Ceausescu adhered ever more closely to the communist orthodoxy of centralized administration at home. His secret police maintained rigid controls over free speech and the media and tolerated no internal dissent or opposition. In an effort to pay off the large foreign debt that his government had accumulated through its mismanaged industrial ventures in the 1970s, Ceausescu in 1982 ordered the export of much of the country's agricultural and industrial production.

The resulting drastic shortages of food, fuel, energy, medicines, and other basic necessities drove Romania from a state of relative economic well-being to near starvation. Ceausescu also instituted an extensive personality cult and appointed his wife, Elena, and many members of his extended family to high posts in the government and party. Among his grandiose and impractical schemes was a plan to bulldoze thousands of Romania's villages and move their residents into new apartment buildings. Ceausescu's regime collapsed after he ordered his security forces to fire on anti-government demonstrators in the city of Timisoara on December 17, 1989.

The demonstrations spread to Bucharest and on December 22 the Romanian army defected to the demonstrators. That same day Ceausescu and his wife fled the capital in a helicopter but were captured and taken into custody by the armed forces. On December 25, the couple were hurriedly tried and convicted by a special military tribunal on charges of mass murder and other crimes. Ceausescu and his wife were then shot by firing squad.

The Charge

The nations are crying for political governance that will release the greatness of a people and not sabotage it. This cry has led to mass protests like the Arab Spring on every continent in the last five years.

If you are called to political leadership discover your God-given assignment, develop the gift within you and become a political world changer.

End Notes

1. Address by the Rt. Hon. Owen Arthur, Prime Minister, on the occasion of the unveiling of the statue of the Right Excellent Errol Barrow – National Hero, Independence Square, January 21, 2007. Prime Minister's Office

2. The history guide lectures on 20th Century Europe Nicolae Ceauşescu. www.historyguide.com

CHAPTER SEVEN

THE DYNAMICS OF ENTREPRENEURIAL LEADERSHIP

Entrepreneurial Leadership creates influence through the income stream it produces by selling goods and services that meet the needs of people.

Entrepreneurs are men and women who sell goods and services to people at a profit.

CREATION OF JOBS

Entrepreneurs are the backbone of the economies of nations. Their enterprises create hundreds of millions of jobs on the earth. When you find societies in which entrepreneurial ideas and the way of the entrepreneur is not celebrated, poverty is a feature of that society.

These Entrepreneur Leaders come in four categories:

1. **Self-Employed Entrepreneurs**

   These are those whose goods and services provide employment for themselves.

2. **Single Business Entrepreneurs**
   These are gifted to create a single business that can stay as a small business or grow and become a medium or large scale business.

3. **The Serial Entrepreneur**
   These are gifted to create multiple businesses ranging from two to hundreds depending on their leadership gifting and ability.

4. **The Investor Entrepreneur**
   These have money to invest and are gifted in putting their capital to work investing in stocks, real estate or businesses.

LEADERS IN INNOVATION

Innovation is thinking 'outside the box' of history to find new solutions, products and services to solve old problems. Entrepreneurial leaders excel in this way. Much of the innovation in this world like the cell phone, the airplane, the ship, the car, the light bulb and motor cycle have been driven by people in search of solutions to problems for others, that can then be turned into an enterprise. Life would be very boring without these entrepreneurs.

The proliferation of new products coming out every month is due to their passion. They are the great funders of research into new technologies that can add value to people with the desire of making a profit.

Great entrepreneurs have a healthy balance between selling goods and services that add value to people and making a profit.

ISAAC: AN ENTREPRENEUR THAT BECAME AN ECONOMIC POWERHOUSE

"Then Isaac sowed in that land, and reaped in the same year a hundredfold; and the LORD blessed him. The man began to prosper, and continued prospering until he became very prosperous; For he had possessions of flocks and possessions of herds and a great number of servants. So the Philistines envied him. Now the Philistines had stopped up all the wells which his father's servants had dug in the days of Abraham his father, and they had filled them with earth. And Abimelech said to Isaac, "Go away from us, for you are much mightier than we (Genesis 26:12-16)."

Isaac had an unusual heavenly gift for Entrepreneurial Leadership. He started a family enterprise in the land of the Philistines during a drought and a famine and in spite of not receiving rain, his crops grew. This can be seen in the fact that he was the only person successfully growing crops during the time of famine and had a monopoly in the food market.

The scriptures revealed that he became great and created employment as he had a great store of servants. How did he do this? Did it happen supernaturally or was he given a supernatural breakthrough idea from God? As we study the scriptures we notice the following pattern; Isaac's servants digging for water in the wells of Abraham.

"And Isaac digged again the wells of water...And Isaac's servants digged in the valley, and found there a well of springing water. And they digged another well...And he removed from thence, and

digged another well...And he built an altar there, and called upon the name of the LORD, and pitched his tent there: and there Isaac's servants digged a well. And it came to pass the same day, that Isaac's servants came, and told him concerning the well which they had digged, and said unto him, we have found water (Genesis 26:17-22)."

Jewish history tells us that Isaac piped that water to his crops in some form of irrigation by a divine idea, and as a result he became so wealthy that his financial power intimidated a nation. Isaac is a great example that through divine ideas, faith and hard work, an entrepreneur can create goods and services that add value to people lives plus open up employment opportunities for others. You can do the same if you are called to this sphere of Entrepreneurial Leadership.

DEMETRIUS: A BUSINESS TYCOON WHO BECAME RICH FROM IDOLATRY

"And about that time there arose a great commotion about the Way. For a certain man named Demetrius, a silversmith, who made silver shrines of Diana, brought no small profit to the craftsmen. He called them together with the workers of similar occupation, and said: "Men, you know that we have our prosperity by this trade. Moreover, you see and hear that not only at Ephesus, but throughout almost all Asia, this Paul has persuaded and turned away many people, saying that they are not gods which are made with hands. So not only is this trade of ours in danger of falling into disrepute, but also the temple of the great goddess Diana may be despised and her magnificence destroyed, whom all Asia and the world worship.

Now when they heard this, they were full of wrath and cried out, saying, "Great is Diana of the Ephesians!" So the whole city was filled with confusion, and rushed into the theater with one accord, having seized Gaius and Aristarchus, Macedonians, Paul's travel companions. And when Paul wanted to go in to the people, the disciples would not allow him. Then some of the officials of Asia, who were his friends, sent to him pleading that he would not venture into the theater. Some, therefore, cried one thing and some another, for the assembly was confused, and most of them did not know why they had come together. And they drew Alexander out of the multitude, the Jews putting him forward. And Alexander motioned with his hand, and wanted to make his defense to the people. But when they found out that he was a Jew, all with one voice cried out for about two hours, "Great is Diana of the Ephesians!

And when the city clerk had quieted the crowd, he said: "Men of Ephesus, what man is there who does not know that the city of the Ephesians is temple guardian of the great goddess Diana, and of the image which fell down from Zeus? Therefore, since these things cannot be denied, you ought to be quiet and do nothing rashly. For you have brought these men here who are neither r o b b e r s   o f t e m p l e s   n o r   b l a s p h e m e r s   o f   y o u r   g o d d e s s . Therefore, if Demetrius and his fellow craftsmen have a case against anyone, the courts are open and there are proconsuls. Let them bring charges against one another. But if you have any other inquiry to make, it shall be determined in the lawful assembly. For we are in danger of being called in question for today's uproar, there being no reason which we may give to account for this disorderly gathering." And when he had said these things, he dismissed the assembly (Acts 19:23-41)."

Money is simply a medium of exchange for goods and services, whether these services add value to people or strip value and dignity from people. Mr. Demetrius was an entrepreneur who created wealth from people's sin. He built silver shrines to satisfy the appetites of idol worshippers of the goddess Diana. There are many entrepreneurs today in nations that are after the order of Demetrius.

They create goods and services that they sell for a profit to meet the needs of people's sin appetite. In doing so, some build companies that provide supply for the sinful desires of people into enterprises that contribute taxes and jobs to the national economy. This was the case with Demetrius and is the case of many entrepreneurs.

There is an old adage that states, 'he who has the gold makes the rules.' It is time for a new generation of Christian Entrepreneurial Leaders to rise and create tens, hundreds and thousands of jobs producing goods and services that add value to their nation.

ROBERT G. LETOURNEAU: GOD'S BUSINESSMAN (1888-1969)

One of the most amazing 'rags to riches' stories is the life of RG LeTourneau, as told in his biography, '*Mover of Mountains and Men.*' LeTourneau began his career in obscurity in Stockton, California, where his first job was transporting earth to 'level out' farmland. His frustrations with moving dirt drove him to find a better, more efficient way. In 1922, he constructed the first all-welded scraper that was lighter, stronger and less expensive than any other machine.

LeTourneau became the greatest obstacle mover in history by building huge earth-moving machines. During World War II, he produced 70% of all the army's earth-moving machinery. He spoke of God as the Chairman of his Board.

As a multi-millionaire, LeTourneau gave 90% of his profit to God's work and kept only 10% for himself. A special friend of Billy Graham in his early days, LeTourneau designed a portable dome building intended for Graham's crusades. He also founded a university that is thriving to this day. LeTourneau said that the money came in faster than he could give it away. LeTourneau was convinced that he could not out-give God. "I shovel it out," he would say, "and God shovels it back, but God has a bigger shovel."

Many people see LeTourneau as one of the most influential people of the past hundred years. As the Father of the Modern Earthmoving Industry, he was responsible for 299 inventions. These inventions included the bulldozer, scrapers of all sorts, dredgers, portable cranes, rollers, dump wagons, bridge spans, logging equipment, mobile sea platforms for oil exploration, the electric wheel, and many others. He introduced into the earthmoving and material-handling industry, the rubber tire which today is almost universally accepted. He invented and developed the electric wheel. His life's verse was Matthew 6:33, "Seek ye first the kingdom of God and His righteousness and all these things shall be added unto you."

LeTourneau's example reminds us that we too can be Mountain Movers. As the Lord said in Matthew 17:20, "I tell you the truth, if you have faith as small as a mustard seed, you can say to this mountain, move from here to there and it will move. Nothing will be impossible for you." RG LeTourneau once said, "You will never know what you can accomplish until you say a great big yes to the Lord." My prayer is that God may raise up many creative leaders who like LeTourneau, will be movers of mountains and people.

LARRY FLINT: A KING OF THE ENTERPRISE OF SEXUAL IMMORALITY

The porn industry has become a billion-dollar industry and one of its movers and shakers is Larry Flint. He has an estimated net worth of $400 million and created a global enterprise from selling to the young and old, the product of sexual sin through pornography and related activities.

He has influenced millions of people in this generation and is featured in the film, '*The People vs.* Larry Flynt *(1996).* '

He is the founder of Larry Flynt Publications, a company whose holdings include:

1. Pornographic magazines with a circulation of 3 million at its peak

2. Video studios that produce pornographic movies

3. A casino

4. High end strip clubs

5. A Hollywood store

He is a true businessman whose products and services have advanced the kingdom of darkness in the earth.

The Charge
When Godly Entrepreneurial Leaders emerge they help lift the masses out of lack and add great value to nations. I believe that men and women with the entrepreneurial gifting of Abraham, Isaac, Jacob and

Solomon will emerge out of the church in this hour and save the economies of cities and nations. What a great moment in history to be a Kingdom Entrepreneurial Leader.

I see you rising to become an economic deliverer to many.

End Notes

1. RG LeTourneau: Mover of Men and Mountains Autobiography (Prentice-Hall 1960, 1967; Reprint Moody Press 1967, 1972)

2. Wikipedia: Larry Flint

CHAPTER EIGHT

THE DYNAMICS OF MILITARY AND LAW ENFORCEMENT LEADERSHIP

Military and Law Enforcement Leadership is empowering leadership that mobilizes people to advance or defend those strategic interests and laws of a people group, through the threat or use of lethal force.

Life is warfare and peace is the reward of winning a war. Revelation 12, i s an amazing scripture which reads, "And there was war in heaven and Michael and his angels fought against the dragon and his angels."
If there was war in heaven and Michael and his angels had to fight against Satan and his angels to win the war, know with a certainty that there will be wars and rumors of wars on the earth.

I reiterate that there can be no lasting peace except nations win wars. We were born into a world where there is conflict between good and evil. There was good and evil in the realm of the spirit before the human race was created and we became part of a fight that started long before time began.

This fight determines the borders of nations, the ethnic balance of nations, the economic opportunities of people groups and the safety in your neighborhood. This war is fought on many different levels, and at each level God and Satan have their leaders that take or defend territory through the seed of battle. This is illustrated in the reign of David and Solomon. Solomon had a reign of peace and prosperity because his father David had won all the decisive wars and had subdued the Philistines securing the borders of Israel and the safety of his people.

Let us examine the different levels of warfare that Military leaders are actually positioned to lead. Military leadership does not exist without the threat and the use of lethal force. David could not secure the borders of Israel without the killing of many people. This is the reality and it is not relegated just to the Old Testament.

1. Territorial Warfare.

2. Internal Security Warfare.

3. Citizen-Safety Warfare.

TERRITORIAL WARFARE

The defense of the territory of a nation is crucial to its national security. When a nation does not have military leadership that can adequately defend its territorial sovereignty and its strategic interests, the destiny of that nation will always be in the balance. A great example of this is the nation of Sierra Leone when Foday Sankoh, a rebel leader in partnership with Charles Taylor, the President of Liberia, started making raids within the borders of Sierra Leone and succeeded in annexing the diamond rich border towns. The Sierra Leonean army and its leadership were inadequate to repel the attacks and this led to a civil war that claimed thousands of lives and caused economic and social devastation.

Effective Military Leadership would have prevented this and provided a secure framework for Sierra Leone to grow into a developed country. However, the war knocked the country back many years, as it destroyed the national infrastructure and created a generation of child soldiers.

INTERNAL SECURITY WARFARE

There are always people in groups that want to destabilize governments for their evil intents and create visible or invisible coup d'état's. Military Leadership is also required to protect the executive and legislated branches and the operation of governments from internal military action. Another example of poor military leadership was displayed in the nation of Sierra Leone where a sitting President, Tejan Kabbah, was able to prevent a coup d'état arising from the army by putting the ringleaders in jail.

However, due to totally ineffective internal policing and intelligence, these same ring leaders planned another coup d'état which became successful from inside the very jail itself. The costs of this coup were thousands of lost lives, raped women and economic devastation.

What happened in Sierra Leone was an outpouring of evil that effective Military Leadership and intelligence should have prevented.

Citizen-Safety Warfare

Every society has its fair share of criminals that can only be prevented from doing their criminal work by a robust police force and the threat of being caught.   When policing is weak, criminals reign supreme and they devastate societies with drugs, robbery, violence and rape.   There are cities in the world that have neighborhoods that are ruled by criminals which is due to ineffective police leadership, which is a type of Military Leadership that protects the safety of citizens.

The army, air force, navy and special forces protect the territorial sovereignty and the strategic interest of the country. Intelligence services and paramilitary forces protect the internal security of the country and the police force protects the safety of the citizens.

GIDEON: A MILITARY DELIVERER

"So Gideon and the hundred men who were with him came to the outpost of the camp at the beginning of the middle watch, just as they had posted the watch; and they blew the trumpets and broke the pitchers that were in their hands. Then the three companies blew the trumpets and broke the pitchers—they held the torches in their left hands and the trumpets in their right hands for blowing— and they cried, "The sword of the LORD and of Gideon!" And every man stood in his place all around the camp; and the whole army ran and cried out and fled. When the three hundred blew the trumpets, the LORD set every man's sword against his companion throughout the whole camp; and the army fled to Beth Acacia, toward Zererah, as far as the border of Abel Meholah, by Tabbath (Judges 7:19-22)."

Gideon was a Military Leader with an exceptional gift. He was handpicked by God to deliver the nation of Israel from the Midianites. His leadership was so potent that when he issued the call for the fighting men of Israel to assemble, over 20,000 showed up. The Lord proceeded to tell him that there were too many.

Through a process of divine elimination, Gideon was left with three hundred fighting men. To the casual observer, this seemed odd and might even be considered a suicide mission. However, when you understand the gifting and the anointing that God had put on Gideon for military conquest, you will appreciate why only three hundred human soldiers were required.

The Scriptures tell us that when the battle commenced, the magnitude of Gideon's gift was made manifest. The scripture used the phrase, "the sword of the Lord and the sword of Gideon." It literally meant that when Gideon fought divinely mandated battles, the angels of the Lord fought with him.

In that battle against the Midianites, there were 300 Israeli soldiers who had angels fighting along with them, because the Lord set every man's sword against his companion's throughout the whole camp. This anointing is still available in the earth today and there are men and women who walk in it.

GOLIATH: A MILITARY CHAMPION FROM THE DARK SIDE

"And a champion went out from the camp of the Philistines, named Goliath, from Gath, whose height was six cubits and a span. He had a bronze helmet on his head, and he was armed with a coat of mail, and the weight of the coat was five thousand shekels of bronze. And he had bronze armor on his legs and a bronze javelin between his shoulders. Now the staff of his spear was like a weaver's beam and his iron spearhead weighed six hundred shekels; and a shield-bearer went before him. Then he stood and cried out to the armies of Israel, and said to them, "Why have you come out to line up for battle? Am I not a Philistine, and you the servants of

Saul? Choose a man for yourselves, and let him come down to me. If he is able to fight with me and kill me, then we will be your servants. But if I prevail against him and kill him, then you shall be our servants and serve us." And the Philistine said, "I defy the armies of Israel this day; give me a man, that we may fight together." When Saul and all Israel heard these words of the Philistine, they were dismayed and greatly afraid (1 Samuel 17:4-11)."

Goliath is not the type of warrior that you want to meet on a dark night. He was an imposing, unnatural, and intimidating figure. His presence struck fear in the hearts and minds of Israel's king and soldiers. He was empowered not only by his physical stature and training but also by his gods, which was illustrated when he cursed David by them, who were demons.

It took a man anointed by the Spirit of God to defeat him. There are military figures today that advance the agenda of Satan that are empowered by Satan and can only be defeated by anointed military leaders from the army, navy, air force, para-military intelligence services or police force.

GEORGE WASHINGTON: AN AMERICAN MILITARY DELIVERER

George Washington as a military leader was shaped in part by his upbringing. George Washington spent many days in his youthful years working as a surveyor for Lord Fairfax of England in what is now the State of Virginia. This experience gave him an understanding of the land he would later fight as a soldier, for and against the British.

Washington fought in two famous wars of the 1700s. The first he fought for the British as a Lt. Colonel and later as the Commander of all Virginian troops in the French and Indian War. The second was the Revolutionary War in which he fought as the Commander in Chief of the Continental Army, that would eventually become the army of the great United States of America.

During the French and Indian War, Washington wrote a letter to his mother after a great defeat which not only killed or wounded the bulk of the British soldiers that participated but also killed his General, Edward Braddock. In this letter, Washington explained that two horses were shot from beneath him and that he had four bullet holes in his coat.

There seemed to be a spiritual covering over Washington throughout his soldiering and political career. His wisdom was unmatched by his peers and all who encountered him respected his presence and decision making.

There are few on this planet who can say that men would risk their life to fight for them and their view of current affairs. George Washington was one of the few. His convictions in God and his hope for a free nation empowered Washington to influence those around him in a powerful way.

His influence was so powerful that all who caught a glimpse of his vision sparked into flame their own passion and desire to stand for freedom both politically and religiously, and to fight against the tyranny that opposed that passion and desire. The greatest part was that he not only voiced this influence, he lived it and exemplified it through his actions. He was just a man and he lived with purpose, passion, conviction, bravery, and a humble submission to one higher than himself. He encompassed the ingredients of a true leader and those who chose to follow him consumed all he had to offer.

FODAY SANKOH: A HUMAN BUTCHER FROM HELL

Foday Sankoh was the leader and founder of the Sierra Leone rebel group called Revolutionary United Front (RUF) in the Sierra Leone civil war, that lasted for eleven years starting in 1991 and ending in 2002. An estimated 50,000 people were killed during the war and over 500,000 people were displaced in neighboring countries.

In 1971 Sankoh, who at the time was a corporal in the Sierra Leonean army, was cashiered from the army's signal corps and imprisoned for seven years at the Pademba Road Prison in Freetown for taking part in a mutiny.

On his release, he worked as an itinerant photographer in the south and east of Sierra Leone, eventually coming in contact with young radicals and found his way to Libya for insurgency training in 1988. This was organized by Muammar Gaddafi who also helped to bring Charles Taylor to power.

According to Douglas Farah, "The amputation of the arms and legs of men, women, and children as part of a scorched-earth campaign was designed to take over the region's rich diamond fields and was backed by Gaddafi, who routinely reviewed their progress and supplied weapons."

On their return to Sierra Leone, Sankoh and confederates Rashid Mansaray and Abu Kanu solicited support for an armed uprising to oust the APC government. They then traveled to Liberia, where they reportedly continued recruiting and served with Charles G. Taylor's National Patriotic Front of Liberia (NPFL).

On March 23, 1991, the RUF led by Foday Sankoh and backed by Charles Taylor, launched its first attack in villages in the Kailahun

District in the diamond-rich Eastern Province of Sierra Leone. The RUF became notorious for brutal practices such as mass rapes and amputations during the Civil War.

Sankoh personally ordered many operations including one called "Operation Pay Yourself" that encouraged troops to loot anything they could find. After complaining about such tactics Kanu and Mansaray were summarily executed. In March 1997, Sankoh fled to Nigeria where he was put under house arrest and then imprisoned. From this time until Sankoh's release in 1999, Sam Bockarie performed the task of director of military operations of the RUF. During the eleven-year war, Sankoh broke several promises to stop fighting including the Abidjan Peace Accord and the Lomé Peace Accord signed in 1999.

Eventually, the United Kingdom and ECOMOG intervened with their own small but professional military forces and the RUF was eventually crushed. Sankoh was later arrested after his soldiers gunned down a number of protesters outside his Freetown home in 2000. His arrest led to massive celebrations throughout Sierra Leone.

Sankoh was handed to the British and under jurisdiction of a UN-backed court was indicted on 17 counts for various war crimes, including the use of child soldiers and crimes against humanity. Sankoh died of complications arising from a stroke whilst awaiting trial. In a statement by the UN-backed War Crimes Court, Chief Prosecutor David Crane said that Sankoh's death granted him "a peaceful end that he denied to many others."

However, the story of George Washington illustrates that there are still some people who are anointed like David, Gideon and Samson to win ministry conflicts which cannot be avoided in order for peace and stability to reign in certain regions, like Sierra Leone.

The Charge
If you are called to the sphere of Military and Law Enforcement Leadership, your gift is very precious as wars and rumors of wars continually invade neighborhoods, communities, towns, cities and nations. A world without honorable Military and Law enforcement leaders will be a world of chaos and anarchy where Gods plans will be thwarted.

Always remember that heaven has peace because God our Father won the war. You are anointed to win wars that threaten the destiny of neighborhoods, communities, towns, cities and nations.

Arise and fulfill your calling.

End Notes

1. Foday Sankoh Wikpedia

2. George Washington: www.allabouthistory.org

CHAPTER NINE

THE DYNAMICS OF EDUCATIONAL LEADERSHIP

Educational Leadership develops the potential of multitudes through the teaching of knowledge, ideology and skill development.

The philosophy of the classroom in one generation, is the philosophy of the government in the next. Thought patterns, world views, ideologies, skill development, capacity building and competence development are all the hallmark of Educational Leadership.

Educational leaders are important and found in nurseries, primary and secondary schools, colleges, technical schools and universities. Their roles are diverse and they may take the form of teachers, principals, school administrators, and curriculum developers.

EDUCATORS: TEACH A WORLDVIEW

The Sphere of Educational Leadership is a real battleground in Western Countries today. This is because the lesbian and gay lobby groups have infiltrated the educational system and are introducing curriculum that teach our children what is tantamount to sexual perversion under the guise of sex education.

There is a need for a critical mass of godly Educational leaders to arise and transform the system. When you study the rise of education in North America and Europe, history teaches us that many of the great universities and schools came out of the church. However, many of them have become bastions of the doctrines of demons.

In a university in London, Ontario, one of my team members informed me that one of his professors of Business Ethics told a class that there was no ethics in business; therefore, you just do what you have to do to get what you want.

EDUCATORS: TEACH THE RELEVANT SKILLS REQUIRED TO SOLVE TODAY'S PROBLEMS

The creation and teaching of a skills-development curriculum is one of the pillars of a good education. A 'bad' education teaches skills that are obsolete in today's world. Working as an Employment Officer for the British Civil Service, I regularly met people who were highly qualified in areas that were no longer relevant.

Such a situation occurred to a friend of mine, who had just completed a course in Mechanical Engineering during the time when jobs in many factories had been replaced by computerized equipment. Though highly qualified and very astute in his field, he soon realized that his skills were irrelevant in the job market.

I can also think of a second example of an Automobile Mechanics Course that is run by a college based in the Caribbean, in which students learn how to fix cars. However, the course did not teach students how to fix the cars that are produced today which are mostly run by computers. These students were very frustrated when they completed their studies and found that none of the large garages would hire them because they did not know how to fix cars that had been built in the last five years.

Let us examine a formula that explains the different types of education.

1. Wrong world view + irrelevant skill development = terrible education.

2. Wrong world view + relevant skill development = average education.

3. Biblical world view + irrelevant skill development = poor education.

4. Biblical world view + relevant skill development = great education.

GAMALIEL: A PROFESSOR OF THE LAW OF MOSES AND EDUCATIONAL INFLUENCER

"When they heard this, they were furious and plotted to kill them. Then one in the council stood up, a Pharisee named Gamaliel, a teacher of the law held in respect by all the people, and commanded them to put the apostles outside for a Little while. And he said to them: "Men of Israel, take heed to yourselves what you intend to do regarding these men. For some time ago, Theudas rose up, claiming to be somebody. A number of men, about four hundred, joined him. He was slain, and all who obeyed him were scattered and came to nothing. After this man, Judas of Galilee rose up in the days of the census, and drew away many people after him. He also perished, and

all who obeyed him were dispersed. And now I say to you, keep away from these men and let them alone; for if this plan or this work is of men, it will come to nothing; but if it is of God, you cannot overthrow it—lest you even be found to fight against God." And they agreed with him, and when they had called for the apostles and beaten them, they commanded that they should not speak in the name of Jesus, and let them go (Acts 5:33-40)."

"Brethren and fathers, hear my defense before you now." And when they heard that he spoke to them in the Hebrew language, they kept all the more silent. Then he said: "I am indeed a Jew, born in Tarsus of Cilicia, but brought up in this city at the feet of Gamaliel, taught according to the strictness of our fathers' law, and was zealous toward God as you all are today (Acts 22:1-3)."

Gamaliel was one of the major educational influences during the period of the Book of Acts. He is known for two major things. Firstly, Paul the apostle credits his understanding of the law to the teachings of Gamaliel. He was also a man who taught the 'movers' and 'shakers' of his day.

His significant influence was demonstrated when he intervened on behalf of the apostles. The Council of Pharisees was plotting to kill them and he showed knowledge of the character of God, by advising the Council of Pharisees not to fight the work of the apostles because if it was of God they would not be able to overthrow it but if it was the work of men, it would come to nothing.

ASHPENAZ: EDUCATIONAL LEADER IN IDEAS AND PHILOSOPHIES OF BABYLON

"Then the King instructed Ashpenaz, the master of his eunuchs, to

bring some of the children of Israel and some of the king's descendants and some of the nobles, young men in whom there was no blemish, but good looking, gifted in all wisdom, possessing knowledge and quick to understand, who had ability to serve in the king's palace, and whom they might teach the language and literature of the Chaldeans. And the King appointed for them a daily provision of the King's delicacies and of the wine which he drank, and three years of training for them, so that at the end of that time they might serve before the King. Now, from among those of the sons of Judah were Daniel, Hananiah, Mishael, and Azariah. To them the chief of the eunuchs gave names: he gave Daniel the name Belteshazzar; to Hananiah, Shadrach; to Mishael, Meshach; and to Azariah, Abed-Nego (Daniel1:3-7)."

Ashpenaz was the Chief Eunuch and Educational Leader to the young Hebrew boys. In his teaching, he would have not only taught them the language of the Chaldeans but also the culture, worship and dark arts of the Chaldeans.

This education was partly rejected by Daniel and the three Hebrew boys who chose not to defile themselves with the king's meat. I must say that the king's meat was not the only thing that had the potential to defile, but the literature and ways of the Chaldeans also had the potential to defile.

The book of Daniel reveals that the four Hebrew boys chose not to be defiled but to glorify God in their captivity.

DR. DAVID OYEDEPO: A TRANSFORMATIONAL EDUCATIONAL LEADER

Dr. David Oyedepo is Founder and Chancellor of Covenant University, Landmark University, Faith Academy and Kingdom

Heritage Model Schools in the nation of Nigeria.

Dr. Oyedepo is a dynamic Minister of the Gospel and educational pioneer who is leading a transformation on the continent of Africa through Christian ministry and education. Landmark University is his most recent educational institution.

Dr. Oyedepo has a focus on assisting the nation of Nigeria and indeed the continent of Africa in self-discovery, so that the region may recover its leading position in education and in civilization as it was in the 15th Century. The goal is to set the pace in making the Nigerian nation fully competitive and profitably engaged with its comparative advantage in human and agricultural resource potentials and development.

Covenant University, an institution he also founded in 2002, is currently pioneering a revolution in education not only in Nigeria but elsewhere on the African Continent.

With the motto, *'Raising a new Generation of Leaders,'* the university was founded on a profound philosophical departure platform of moving Nigeria's education from form to skill, from knowledge to empowerment, from figures to future-building, from legalism to realism, from points to facts and from mathematics to "life-matics."

Apart from the foundational feats achieved by the University, such as being the first private University in Nigeria to have the fastest approval of its application for operating license by the National Universities Commission (NUC); he was also the first in the annals of Nigeria tertiary institutions to start full academic and administrative activities at its permanent site from the inception, with all facilities in place. It is also the first university to have all of its 16 programs presented for accreditation approved by the NUC.

Presently, Covenant University is known as a center of excellence, and like nectar, is attracting the best brains in the land. An acclaimed author and publisher, Dr. Oyedepo has written over 60 titles apart from periodicals. He is also Chairman/Publisher of Dominion Publishing House (DPH), a publishing branch of his ministry. DPH has over 4 million prints in circulation to date. In 1992 it won a Gold Merit Award of the Economic Community of West African State (ECOWAS).

Dr. Oyedepo's dogged commitment to excellence has also won him many honours and awards. These include:

- "The Biographic Centre, Cambridge, "International Who is Who of intellectuals, 13th Edition" of the International Biographical Centre, Cambridge, England.
- "Man of Dignity" by Global Care International, "Frontline Christian Author" by ECOWAS International Gold Award and "Inscribed in the Jerusalem 3000 Scroll #102268".
- "Doctor of Divinity" by Bethel Graduate School of Technology, Riverside, California, USA.
- "Fellow, Nigerian Academy of Education" and "Fellow, Institute of Strategic Management, Nigeria".

JOHN DEWY: FATHER OF PROGRESSIVE EDUCATION AND ADVOCATE OF LIBERALISM

Dewey is lauded as one of the greatest educational influencers of the 20th century. John Dewey, the Father of Modern American Education contributed to the book, "The Humanist Manifesto" in 1933.

No education is complete today without understanding 'The Humanist Manifesto I and II' and tracing the influence of those signers and supporters of the intentions expressed therein.

His theory of experience continues to be much read and discussed not only within education, but also in psychology and philosophy. Dewey's views continue to strongly influence the design of innovative educational approaches, such as in outdoor education, adult training, and experiential therapies.

Dewey became the champion or philosophical father of Experiential Education or as it was then referred to, Progressive Education. But he was also critical of completely "free, student- driven" education because students often do not know how to structure their own learning experiences for maximum benefit.

A product of his impact has been the successful teaching to millions of children that God is imaginary and contrary to "science." To satisfy the fundamental question of "Where did we come from?" children are taught the doctrine of Evolution. The first plank of the 'Humanist Manifesto' states, "Religious humanists regard the universe as self-existing and not created." The second plank states, "Humanism believes that man is a part of nature and that he has emerged as a result of a continuous process."

Educational Leadership affects the trajectory of a nation. We as a church must not fold our hands and give up education to the agents of humanistic doctrines. There has never been a time when godly Educational Leaders are required to bring light and salt to a system in decay and corruption.

The Charge
If you are called to Educational leadership what a great day to be alive. God saves the best for last and the greatest singers, doctors, scientists,

poets, social workers and chefs etc., are going to be your students.

Become a hunter of talent and give the children and youth in your nation an education that will launch them in the trajectory of a positive world changer. Mold their minds for greatness, inspire them by your example and launch them into destiny.

End Notes

1. www.davidoyedepo.org

2. Wikipedia John Dewey

CHAPTER TEN

THE DYNAMICS OF SOCIAL CARE LEADERSHIP

Social Care Leadership influences nations by creating and operating social enterprises and services that meet the practical needs of a society.

Creating social enterprises that meet the practical needs of people is the hallmark of Social Care leadership. These fall into several categories.

Health Care
This includes doctors, nurses, dentists, hospitals and all medical service operations.

Mental Health Care
This service includes psychologists, psychiatrists, psychotherapists, and all mental care personnel.

Child and Youth Care Service
Included in this service are government agencies that deal with adoption, foster care, orphans and the social enterprises, such as, the Girl's Guides and the Boys Scouts.

Elderly Care

This type of service includes government agencies and private enterprises that deal with the care of the elderly.

Financial Safety Net Services

This type of service includes social organizations and government agencies that provide a safety net for those who are going through financial hardships in our society. They provide homeless shelters, local housing, financial assistance, medical assistance, clothing and agencies such as the Salvation Army.

Addiction Care Services

These include government agencies and social organizations that deal with those who are addicted to drugs, alcohol, sex, gambling and other vices, and provide counseling to family members affected by these addictions.

Cultural Care

This service includes organizations and government agencies that care for the artifacts and cultural emblems and art work of a people, such as museums.

Environmental Care

These include government agencies and social organizations that care for our environment such as those involved in the planting of trees, conservation of forests and other similar activities.

DORCAS: A SOCIAL HUMANITARIAN

"At Joppa there was a certain disciple named Tabitha, which is translated Dorcas. This woman was full of good works and charitable deeds which she did. But it happened in those days that she became sick and died. When they had washed her, they laid her in

an upper room. And since Lydda was near Joppa, and the disciples had heard that Peter was there, they sent two men to him, imploring him not to delay in coming to them. Then Peter arose and went with them. When he had come, they brought him to the upper room. And all the widows stood by him weeping, showing the tunics and garments which Dorcas had made while she was with them. But Peter put them all out, and knelt down and prayed. And turning to the body he said, "Tabitha, arise." And she opened her eyes, and when she saw Peter she sat up. Then he gave her his hand and lifted her up; and when he had called the saints and widows, he presented her alive (Acts 9:36-41)."

The life of Dorcas illustrates the principle that when you provide services that meet the needs of people, there will be a human outcry if your lights ever go out. It is important to note that in the ministry of Dorcas, the lights went out permanently when she died.

Her presence and her impact were so missed that Peter the apostle was moved to raise her from the dead, which he did. What did Dorcas really do? She simply met the needs of widows by providing clothing for them plus other charitable deeds. This made her indispensable.

She did not occupy a pulpit ministry but she certainly transformed the lives of people. She was truly a heaven-sent Social leader to the widows who had lost the covering and financial flow that a husband would have provided. She used the gift she had of uncommon compassion and the ability to make clothing for others and turned it into a social enterprise that impacted a town.

If you are called to Social leadership, do not minimize your gift. Use what you have been given and connect it to the uncommon compassion that flows through you and meet the needs of people.

DON AND DEYON STEPHENS: GROUND BREAKING HUMANITARIANS AND SOCIAL ENTREPRENEURS

In 1978, Don and Deyon Stephens, the founders of Mercy Ships began the process of finding a suitable vessel to fulfill the dream in their hearts of a hospital ship serving the world's poor.

After surveying many ships, the *'Anastasis'* (ex Victoria) was selected as the most suitable in relating to fulfilling the objectives laid out in the feasibility study. The purchase of the ship for $1 million was completed on October 5, 1978 through loans.

Don and Deyon began recruiting crew members to staff the ship and to raise the funding to bring the Mercy Ship into compliance with international standards which had recently expired. Four years were required to do this. Ongoing efforts resulted in the transformation of the passenger ship into a hospital ship that served for almost 30 years. The *'Africa Mercy'* replaced the retired *'Anastasis'* in June of 2007, and is the largest charity hospital ship in the world. Following the model of Jesus, the founders of Mercy Ships believe the nature and character of a loving God must be demonstrated both visibly and verbally. The volunteer crew is dedicated to bringing hope and healing to the forgotten poor.

In 2009, the Variety Club's International Humanitarian Award, whose previous winners include Sir Winston Churchill and Audrey Hepburn, was awarded to Don and Deyon Stephens in London. Don Stephens has received the 'Two Hungers Award' and the 'Religious Heritage Award.'

Don is also a Paul Harris Fellow through Rotary. Conversant in German and French, Don lectures internationally and is the author of three books, *'Trial by Trial,'* *'Mandate for Mercy'* and *'Ships of*

Mercy.'

LESBIAN, GAY, BISEXUAL & TRANSGENDER COMMUNITY CENTER: A SOCIAL ENTREPRENEURIAL CENTER FOR THE SATAN'S END TIME MILITANT SODOM AND GOMORRAH AGENDA

Just as we have social entrepreneurs who advance the agenda of God, so are there social entrepreneurs that care for societies and groupings of people that are built around sin. A perfect example of this is the Lesbian, Gay, Bisexual & Transgender Community Center which was established in 1983 in the state of New York. The Lesbian, Gay, Bisexual & Transgender Community Center has grown to become the largest LGBT multi-service organization on the East Coast and second largest LGBT community center in the world. Every week, 6,000 people visit the Center, and more than 300 groups meet there. This is an impressive number.

They provide services that meet and support the aspirations of the LGBT community and they provide meeting space at a very low cost for LGBT advocacy groups and organizations in the world. They have become a command center for the spread of the Sodom and Gomorrah doctrine worldwide.

Groups that meet their plan outreaches and campaigns as far as Uganda, Cameroon and the Middle East. Satan is simply a copycat. He imitates the pattern that God uses to influence the earth, and positions his own leaders in the Twelve Spheres of Leadership.

The Charge
If you are called to become a Social leader you can have a transformative effect on your nation. There are people waiting for the

solutions that you carry. Arise and serve what heaven has given you for them through practical acts of service.

End Notes

1. www.mercyship.org
Don and Deyon Stephens

CHAPTER ELEVEN

THE DYNAMICS OF FAMILY LEADERSHIP

Family Leadership provides vision, guidance, development and resources for the growth and well-being of the immediate and extended family.

Family was the first institution that God created after He made Adam. It is the foundation of civilization. It is the most important center of learning, for in the family environment you do not only learn, but you are affected by the spirit of your family.

Family Leadership is often overlooked in today's society where we expect the church, government agencies, social agencies, educational institutions and the arts and entertainment world to take up the slack for the loss of good leadership in today's families.

Leaders shape the future with ideas, and family leaders shape the future of their families with their ideas, values and convictions. In understanding family leadership, there are four words to examine. These are:

1. Husband

2. Wife

3. Father

4. Mother

As you might have noticed the word child is not in that list. Children do not have a leadership role within a family. They are supposed to be protected, guided and released into their potential from within the family.

HUSBAND

The word 'husband' is an old English word that is clearly not understood by the billions of people who use it. We see a reference to this word in the Book of John 15:1 (KJV) where Jesus said, *"I am the vine and my Father is the husbandman and you are the branches."* It is also used in the Book of James 5:7 (KJV) where it says, *"be patient brethren unto the coming of the Lord, behold the Husbandman waited for the precious fruit of the earth, and has long patience for it, until He receives the early and the latter rain."*

The word husbandman literally means cultivator. It is where we get the word husbandry from which is the art of cultivating crops, breeding and raising livestock.

A husband is a leadership title given to a man who has the commitment and competence to cultivate the best out of a woman called his wife. The fact that a man has a title husband does not mean that he has the ability to cultivate you. He may enjoy your presence but he cannot create an environment for the best in you to emerge. Husbandry is a task that involves skill and a man must not marry a woman that he cannot cultivate into the best version of herself. Having sex with a woman and cultivating her are two different things. Receiving from a woman's hand and cultivating her are two different things.

To single men, I say do not marry a woman you cannot cultivate or who will not receive cultivation from you.

WIFE
The word 'wife' is a leadership title that literally means helper. Eve was created to solve a problem for Adam. A wife is a woman who gives a man wings by her love, service and gifts. She literally gives him wings by solving problems for him. Think about it, in Genesis 2:18 the Lord God said, "It is not good for man to be alone. I will make a help mate for him."

A wife gives a man wings and not weights. A woman can love you and make love to you but with that package could come a 200-pound weight that could send you crashing from your destiny. To women, I say, do not marry until you have developed gifts in you that can solve problems for a man and give him wings.

Do not marry a man that cannot receive your help. There is much to say on this subject and for more wisdom you can get my book, '*Uncommon Men and Distinguished Women.*'

Marriage is therefore intended to be a romantic covenant with a purpose between a male cultivator and a female problem solver. Marriage is not a romantic covenant between a male delinquent and a female problem creator.

What is the difference between mothers and fathers?

The role of a father is to coach his children to reach their potential and give them a good start in life. The role of a mother is to provide modeling and nurture for her children.

WHAT ARE THE DIFFERENT TYPES OF FATHERS?

Absentee Fathers:
They are men whose only contribution to the child is the provision of sperm.

Present but Absent Fathers:
They are men who are physically involved in their children's lives but do not mentor them to reach their potential.

Wicked Fathers:
These are men who abuse their children.

Wise Fathers:
These are men who mentor their children into greatness and leave them an inheritance of wisdom or substance.

Fathers play important roles in the lives of their children.

Coach:
A wise father is the primary coach of his children. He studies their gifts, strengths, and weaknesses and helps them find their place in life.
He teaches them the principles of success, right and wrong, service, relationships, sex, community and money.

Disciplinarian:

He provides appropriate discipline to his children so that their weaknesses do not dominate their adult lives and sabotage their happiness, relationships, and success.

Warrior:
He fights and wins certain battles so that his children never have to fight them.

Financier:
He finances his children's welfare until they become fully grown adults and may continue to help them with education and other ventures according to his wealth.

Inheritance:
He provides his children and grandchildren with a great start in life by giving them wisdom, connections, property, money or other assets when they step out of the protection of his home.

Responsibility:
He does not irresponsibly father children with women whom he does not intend to marry. The emotional and financial welfare of his children is a top priority of his life and an issue of honour.

In addition, fathers provide their sons and daughters with the following:

BOYS

1. A model of manhood.

2. Joint recreational pleasure.

3. Education on sex and romance.

4. A listening ear from a male perspective.

GIRLS

1. Male validation of their value and promise.

2. Male education.

3. Protection.

THE ROLE OF MOTHERING

An uncommon woman nurtures and mentors her children for distinction. Motherhood is one the greatest responsibilities known to man. It involves carrying the seed of human life in your womb to full term and nurturing and mentoring the child to distinction.

Uncommon motherhood is based on three foundations which are listed below:

1. The kind of mother you are committed to be to your child.

2. Providing a nurturing environment for the child.

3. Mentoring your child to understand life, develop good character, and maximize their gifts.

Great mothers are great because they have decided to be so and understand the uniqueness and potential of the children they parent.

They are committed to be:

- ☐ Givers.
- ☐ Listeners.
- ☐ Encouragers.
- ☐ Good examples.
- ☐ Protectors of their children's weaknesses.
- ☐ Builders of their children's strengths.

They are committed to the uncommon mother's work and creating an environment that has an atmosphere free of spiritual, mental and emotional poison for their children.

They understand that children like young plants, need the rain and sunshine of love, joy and peace to bloom. They study their children to know their gifts, strengths, weaknesses and vulnerabilities.

They teach life-wisdom and with laser precision work out potential destroying tendencies in their young. They feed their children's potential and help them develop their gifts.

The Charge
Great family leadership requires understanding of the roles of husband, father, mother and wife and using your influence to advance the agenda of God for your family. If you are a husband reading this book, I encourage you to do your best to cultivate your wife, thereby enabling her to be the best version of herself; and if you are a wife reading this book, I encourage you to be a problem-solver for your husband giving him wings to fulfill his destiny.

If you are a father, I encourage you to coach your children into the greatest version of themselves, and if you are a mother I encourage you to nurture and nourish your children into their full potential.

The spirit of your family will affect your life, so do whatever it takes to cause it to be a spirit of love, joy, peace, faith and vision.

CHAPTER TWELVE

THE DYNAMICS OF JUDICIAL LEADERSHIP

Judicial Leadership influences nations by creating, interpreting, advocating and enforcing the laws that govern the life of a nation.

In my study of the Word of God, I realize that one of God's titles is the 'Judge of all the Earth'. Our heavenly Father has a judicial nature. (Revelation 20:11-15). Isaiah 33:22, *"For the LORD is our judge, the LORD is our lawgiver, the LORD is our king; he will save us."*

Our God is a Lawgiver which means He creates laws that establish order that when followed, produces rewards and when broken produces negative consequences. He is also the Judge and decides the rewards for following His law and punishment for breaking His law.

The Kingdom of Heaven is operated on laws and because we are made in the image and likeness of God, the order in our societies is held together by the laws that our judicial leaders create. Satan understands this and he also operates as a lawgiver. He inspires men and women to create laws that release his order, which is to kill, steal, and destroy.

The church as a whole has not understood this and is only now realizing that within the last 50 years. Satan sowed tares of evil men and women into the legal system who would create, advance, legislate and interpret laws to advance the agenda of Satan in many regions including America, Canada, Europe, Africa, the Middle East and South America amongst others.

There are laws and statute books today, that are designed to protect the operations of Satan in nations. In some cities Satan has succeeded in assembling a critical mass of demonically- controlled Judicial Leaders. They highjack the democratic will of the people and pass laws against the wishes of the majority in areas like same sex marriage, taking prayer out of schools, legalizing drug use and the list goes on.

A classic example of this is the ruling in the Supreme Court case that took prayer out of American schools and created such an environment that young teenagers can come into school with guns and open fire killing their peers.

These schools have armed guards who provide security and some of them even have detectors to search for weapons. This did not happen by mistake. A critical mass of Judicial leaders operated against the wishes of parents, teachers and governors in the United States of America and legislated against prayer and a strong Christian witness in schools.

It is a well-known fact that the founding fathers in the USA were for the most part, godly men who used the Bible's principles to construct the Constitution and the Declaration of Independence. Any unbiased American historian knows that the Bible has had a much greater influence in the shaping of the foundation of this nation than is being currently taught in schools.

The United States has laws on the books that enforce punishment on those who would assault and rape women, those who would murder, those who would steal and lie. The source of these laws came directly from the Bible and was given for the protection of society. Many of them can be found in the Old Testament book of Deuteronomy.

Other examples of laws taken directly from the Bible are laws regarding bankruptcy, laws in our courts that demand   witnesses to a crime before one can be convicted, and laws that demand just weights for commerce.

Many of the original laws that America's Judicial System upheld were taken directly from the Bible. Many of these throughout the years have now been altered or abandoned to the detriment of the nation. The present day judicial system has now drifted away from its original intents of protecting the innocent, the unjustly accused and convicting the wicked so they will not harm others.

Today, the Judicial system is being exploited by many lawyers, as well as people who want to use the legal system for personal gain beyond what would be a fair settlement. They are seeking outlandish judgments that in the end all the people will pay for. Through unfair settlements in these kinds of suits, the lawyers are the ones most rewarded.   Protection of the innocent, in many cases, has been overruled while criminals are not justly dealt with.

Quick punishment for the guilty has been abandoned, as court appeals and delays stretch into costly and lengthy trials that last for years at the public's expense. We need to return to Biblical principles and once again shape our laws accordingly if we desire to see justice in our land. In 2 Samuel 23:3, the God of Israel said, "The Rock of Israel spake to me, He that ruleth over men must be just, ruling in the fear of God."

JUDICIAL TREASON

Engel v. Vitale, 370 U.S. 421 (1962), was a landmark United States Supreme Court case that determined that it is unconstitutional for state officials to compose an official school prayer and encourage its recitation in public schools.

The case was taken to court by the families of public school students in New Hyde Park, New York who complained that the voluntary prayer to "Almighty God" contradicted their religious beliefs. They were supported by groups opposed to the school prayer including Rabbinical organizations, Ethical Culture, and Judaic organizations.

The prayer in question was:

Almighty God, we acknowledge our dependence upon Thee, and we beg Thy blessings upon us, our parents, our teachers and our country. Amen.

The plaintiffs argued that opening the school day with such a prayer violates the Establishment Clause of the First Amendment to the United States Constitution (as applied to the states through the Fourteenth), which says in part, "Congress shall make no law respecting an establishment of religion".

The governments of twenty-two states signed on to an *amicus curiae* brief, urging affirmation of the New York Court of Appeal's decision that upheld the constitutionality of the prayer. The American Ethical Union, the American Jewish Committee and the Synagogue each submitted briefs urging the Court to instead reverse and rule that the prayer was unconstitutional.

In an opinion delivered by Justice Hugo Black, the Court ruled that government-written prayers were not to be recited in public schools and were an unconstitutional violation of the Establishment Clause. This was decided in a vote of 6-1, because before the decision could be announced, Justice Felix Frankfurter suffered a cerebral stroke that forced him to retire, and Justice Byron White took no part in the case.

The Court explained the importance of separation between church and state by giving a lengthy history of the issue beginning with the 16th century in England. It then stated that school's prayer is a religious activity by the very nature of it being a prayer, and that prescribing such a religious activity for school children violates the Establishment Clause. The program created by government officials to promote a religious belief was therefore constitutionally impermissible.

The Court rejected the defendant's arguments that people are not asked to respect any specific established religion and that the prayer is voluntary. The Court held that the mere promotion of a religion is sufficient to establish a violation, even if that promotion is not coercive. The Court further held that, the fact that the prayer is vaguely worded enough not to promote any particular religion is not a sufficient defense, as it still promotes a family of religions (those that recognize "Almighty God"), which still violates the Establishment Clause.

Engel became the basis for several subsequent decisions limiting government-directed prayer in school. In *Wallace v. Jaffree* (1985), the Supreme Court ruled Alabama's law permitting one minute for prayer or meditation was unconstitutional. In *Lee v. Weisman* (1992), the court prohibited clergy-led prayer at high school graduation ceremonies. *Lee v. Weisman*, in turn, was a basis for *Santa Fe ISD v.*

Doe (2000), in which the Court extended the ban to school sanctioning of *student*-led prayer at high school football games.

SAMUEL: A RIGHTEOUS JUDICIAL LEADER

"And Samuel judged Israel all the days of his life. He went from year to year on a circuit to Bethel, Gilgal, and Mizpah, and judged Israel in all those places. But he always returned to Ramah, for his home was there. There he judged Israel, and there he built an altar to the LORD (1Samuel 7:15-17)."

JOEL AND ABIJAH: ENEMIES OF JUSTICE

"Now it came to pass when Samuel was old that he made his sons judges over Israel. The name of his firstborn was Joel, and the name of his second, Abijah; they were judges in Beersheba. But his sons did not walk in his ways; they turned aside after dishonest gain, took bribes, and perverted justice (1Samuel 8: 1-3)."

When examining the scriptures of godly and ungodly Judicial leaders, it is discovered that both types of leadership were operating within the household of Samuel. In the days of Samuel, there were some prophets and priests that operated as Judicial leaders and interpreted God's laws to exercise judgment in the cases and disputes that people brought to them.

Samuel was righteous and he decreed judgments based on the facts and correct interpretation of the judicial laws of God to Israel. His sons, Joel and Abjah, however, were preventers of justice and their judgments were influenced by special interest groups who gave them bribes and they opened the door to injustice reigning in the jurisdiction in which they had authority.

The Charge
If you are called to the sphere of Judicial Leadership, you have a heavenly calling. The Heavenly Father is a Judge and Lawgiver whilst Jesus Christ is an advocate for the elect in the court of heaven. Arise in this understanding of your noble profession and represent the interests of the Kingdom of God in the judiciary and nation.

End Notes

1. Wikipedia Engel V Vitale

CHAPTER THIRTEEN

THE DYNAMICS OF MEDIA LEADERSHIP

Media Leadership influences nations by selecting, amplifying and distributing the stories, ideas and events that create the information that most people use to make decisions.

The God of creation is the One who invented the media. He uses the media so well that His thoughts, philosophies and acts are recorded in a Book called the Bible that is the number one best-selling book of all times. That is the optimum use of media. The reason we know about Abraham, Isaac and Jacob is because someone put it on a scroll which became a Book, then an audio tape following with CD, DVD, and movie and internet distribution.

God's Word is spread in the earth through His media leaders like Dr. Luke who wrote the Book of Luke and the Book of Acts. The Book of Luke gives us the most comprehensive account of the birth, life and ministry of Jesus Christ. The Book of Acts is an account of how the early disciples carried out the commission of Jesus, which sets the standard for us today. What would the world be like today without the media leadership of Dr. Luke?

He continues to shape and influence the destiny of nations through his historical account of the acts of the Holy Spirit in the lives of the early apostles and his in-depth exposé on the ministry of Jesus.

Satan also has his media leaders who capture ancient satanic wisdom in scrolls, books, CDs, DVDs, videos, films and the internet and distribute it to the world, which is illustrated in the scripture Exodus 7:8- 13:

"Then the LORD spoke to Moses and Aaron, saying, "When Pharaoh speaks to you, saying, 'Show a miracle for yourselves,' then you shall say to Aaron, 'Take your rod and cast it before Pharaoh, and let it become a serpent.'" So Moses and Aaron went in to Pharaoh, and they did so, just as he LORD commanded.

And Aaron cast down his rod before Pharaoh and before his servants, and it became a serpent. But Pharaoh also called the wise men and the sorcerers; so the magicians of Egypt, they also did in like manner with their enchantments. For every man threw down his rod, and they became serpents. But Aaron's rod swallowed up their rods. And Pharaoh's heart grew hard, and he did not heed them, as the LORD had said."

This dark satanic wisdom that was used by the enchanters of Egypt was not lost. It has been recorded and handed down from generation to generation and put on all types of media platforms to educate men and women in evil.

Let us study further, the four pillars of Media Leadership.

1. Select stories, ideas and events
2. Amplifying stories, ideas and events.
3. Distributing stories, ideas and event information.

4. Create the information flow that most people use to make decisions.

SELECT STORIES, IDEAS AND EVENTS

There are many stories, ideas and events that have happened in the past and are still happening today. Media houses determine which ones to select based on their motivations. They can decide to overlook the fact that 30 000 young people are bullied every day for being overweight and having problems with their teeth and choose to focus on the fifty people that are bullied every day for having a different sexual orientation.

AMPLIFYING STORIES, IDEAS AND EVENTS

As the Holy Spirit was teaching me on Media leadership, He explained to me that Media Leadership is simply a glorified human PA system. What does a PA system do? It picks up the voice of someone and sends it, using sound waves, to a larger group of people with the person not having to change the loudness of his voice.

An example of amplifying something noteworthy is the Teach me to Cook Program. The theme of the program focuses on a housewife teaching her daughter how to cook in their kitchen. Through satellite and cable TV it is then amplified to a world-wide audience. This is how the porn industry operates.

An example of amplifying something evil can be seen in the making of pornographic movies. A group can decide to have an orgy, record it and turn to a TV program that is distributed to millions of home through satellite and cable TV. One million people can watch their sinful deeds and become negatively influenced by it.

DISTRIBUTING STORIES, IDEAS AND EVENTS

The media decides what it chooses to distribute based on its ideology and motivation. This was illustrated to me one day when there was a march of multiple thousands of people against abortion in Canada.

The major media houses chose not to show the mass of people marching against abortion but chose to find a fringe group that had about fifty people, who looked like they had not had a bath for one week and were not articulate. They asked them why they were there and they proceeded to do a poor job of communicating the principles of God on the protection of human rights.

That is the power of Media leadership. It is important that you do not swallow everything that the media tells you. I recall the of disservice a British media house when they interviewed a great servant of the Lord, Dr. Morris Cerrulo. When they aired it on TV they made the lighting very dark and made him look like a mafia leader. That was intentional, wicked and designed to sabotage the agenda that God entrusted to this man.

CREATE THE INFORMATION FLOW THAT MOST PEOPLE USE TO MAKE DECISIONS

In today's world most people do not have time to think for themselves, so they listen to the views espoused on their favourite TV shows and radio programs and use the information to make decisions in their life.

God has always used the media and He is calling for a critical mass of

Media leaders to rise up out of the church and select, amplify and distribute stories, ideas and events that advance the agenda of God on the earth.

Tim LaHaye is one of the authors of *'Left Behind',* a series of 16 best-selling novels that deal with the end times. The series has been adapted into three action thriller films with the fourth being discussed by Cloud Ten Pictures. The films are *Left Behind: The Movie, Left Behind II:Tribulation force* and *Left Behind: World at War.* The series also inspired the PC game "Left Behind: Eternal Forces" and its sequels, "Left Behind: Tribulation Forces" and "Left Behind 3: Rise of the Anti- Christ".

Tim LaHaye's Media leadership has amplified and distributed the revelation of the coming of the Lord to this generation in a dramatic way.

THE HUFFINGTON POST: AN ADVOCATE FOR HUMANISTIC VIEWS

The Huffington Post is an American news website and blog founded by Arianna Huffington, Kenneth Lerer, Andrew Breitbart, and Jonah Peretti, featuring columnists and various news sources. The site offers news, blogs, and original content, and covers politics, business, entertainment, technology, popular media, lifestyle, culture, comedy, healthy living, women's interest and local news.

The Huffington Post was launched on May 9, 2005, as a liberal/left commentary outlet. On February 7, 2011, AOL acquired the mass market *'Huffington Post'* for US$315 million, making Arianna Huffington Editor-in-Chief of The Huffington Post Media Group. In 2012, *'The Huffington Post'* was the first commercially run native digital media enterprise to win a Pulitzer Prize. *The co-founder of The Huffington Post*, Arianna Huffington, was named as number 12 in Forbes' first ever list of the Most Influential Women in Media in 2009. She has also moved up to number 42 in the Guardian's Top 100 in Media List. *Huffington Post* is a progressive liberal advocacy media company and its lens is secular humanistic and anti-evangelical. It is also very militant in its advocacy for Lesbian, Gay bisexual and transgender policies.

The Charge

If you are called to the sphere of Media leadership what a great day to be alive. Never before in the history of the world have we had the opportunity to select divine ideas and stories of what God and good people are doing and distribute it to globally. So purpose in your heart to give truth, good stories and divine ideas a platform and expose the evil of the works of darkness. I know you can!

End Notes

1. Jon Bekken, "Advocacy Newspapers," chapter in Sterling, Christopher H.(2009). *Encyclopedia of Journalism*. SAGE Publications. p. 32. ISBN 0-7619-2957-6.
2. Wikipedia Tim LaHaye

3. Wikipedia Huffington Post

CHAPTER FOURTEEN

THE DYNAMICS OF ARTS & ENTERTAINMENT LEADERSHIP

Arts and Entertainment Leadership influences nations by creating the artistic products, entertainment, music and sporting activities that nations celebrate.

Arts and Entertainment Leaders create the products and experiences that nations celebrate. What is unique about this sphere of leadership is that what one nation celebrates, another nation might despise. An example of this can be seen in the game of cricket, which is one of my favorite sports. I have never shouted, screamed, jumped and danced at any entertainment as I did during a test match between Australia and the West Indies with star batsman, Brian Lara, at the crease.

I can still remember the cheering, the nervousness and the excitement as he led the West Indies to a historic win at the Kensington Oval in Barbados. However, the game of cricket which I love and which millions of people with various nationalities around the world celebrate might mean absolutely nothing to you.

THE 12 SPHERES OF LEADERSHIP

This is the mystery of Arts and Entertainment leadership. In many countries around the world where cricket is celebrated, an influential cricketer's ideas, values and agenda will also be celebrated and adopted by some of his followers.

However, in a nation where cricket is not celebrated, he will not have the same influence. Life was not meant to be serious all the time, and Arts and Entertainment leaders provide the necessary recreation that is needed. As you can imagine, there are Godly Arts and Entertainment leaders as well as Satanic Arts and Entertainment leaders.

A GREAT DANCER FROM THE KINGDOM OF DARKNESS

The best illustration in the scriptures that I have seen of this is the story of Herodias daughter, the woman who danced her way into significant national influence.

"At that time Herod the tetrarch heard the report about Jesus and said to his servants, "This is John the Baptist; he is risen from the dead, and therefore these powers are at work in him." For Herod had laid hold of John and bound him, and put him in prison for the sake of Herodias, his brother, Philip's wife. Because John had said to him, "It is not lawful for you to have her." And although he wanted to put him to death, he feared the multitude, because they counted him as a prophet. But when Herod's birthday was celebrated, the daughter of Herodias danced before them and pleased Herod. Therefore, he promised with an oath to give her whatever she might ask.

So she, having been prompted by her mother, said, "Give me John the Baptist's head here on a platter." And the king was sorry; nevertheless, because of the oaths and because of those who sat with him, he commanded it to be given to her. So he sent and had John beheaded in prison. And his head was brought on a platter and given to the girl, and she brought it to her mother. Then his disciples came and took away the body and buried it, and went and told Jesus (Matt 14:1-12)."

Let us examine this story in more detail:

Herod had a birthday party and during the festivities, a woman made a grand introduction. She was the daughter of his wife. She must have been quite a beauty to look upon and when she started to dance her moves made the king so happy that he promised with an oath to give her whatever she might ask. This was when the demonic agenda behind this Arts and Entertainment leader came into effect.

She asked for the head of John the Baptist who Jesus said was the greatest man born of a woman. Arts and Entertainment leaders create pleasure for others and then leverage the influence that pleasure creates, to advance an agenda that might be ungodly or demonic.

They have an ability to bring pleasure to the highest influencers in society like Herod and to the least.

They have an ability to make people feel pleasure. They come in all different categories:

1. Singers

2. Musicians

3. Comedians

4. Dancers

5. Movie and TV personalities

6. Sports personalities

7. Poets

8. Music and movies producers and directors

9. Artists and sculptures

In understanding arts and entertainment leadership, it is important to see that the influence that these leaders have is in direct proportion to the recreational pleasures they create for others. This pleasure could be the pleasures of sin or clean, good, recreational pleasure.

Satan who had a musical calling based on his design revealed in the Book of Ezekiel 28:12-18, has an intuitive understanding of the power to give sinful or righteous pleasure. He has used these leaders, like the daughter of Herodias to behead the influence of godly spiritual leaders.

What does this mean? There was a time in our world when godly Spiritual leaders and their preaching, teaching and writings created the moral climate that many nations function in. This, however, has changed in some nations due to Arts and Entertainment leaders like:

THE BEATLES: A BAND THAT CHANGED THE VALUES OF A GENERATION AND MADE SIN POPULAR AND REBELLION FASHIONABLE.

The Beatles was a band that changed the morals of a generation. They broke new ground in the Arts and Entertainment industry as they pushed the envelope and took what was forbidden and through lyrics made it popular. They took what preachers called sin and made it the 'in thing' to do. Their impact was undeniable on the moral climate of the English-speaking Europe and North America.

The Beatles is the best-selling band in history with estimated sales of over one billion units. They have had more number-one albums on the UK charts and have held the top spot longer than any other musical act. According to the RIAA, they have sold more albums in the US than any other artist, and in 2008 they topped *Billboard* magazine's list of the all-time most successful Hot 100 artists.

As of 2012, they hold the record for most number one hits on the Hot 100 chart with 20. They have received seven Grammy Awards from the American National Academy of Recording Arts and Sciences and 15 Ivor Novello Awards from the British Academy of Songwriters, Composers and Authors. They were collectively included in *Time Magazine's* compilation of the 20th century's 100 most influential people.

They opened the way for rock starts, rap artists, pop artists and hip-hop artists, who have influenced millions of people and desensitized them to sinful experiences through their music, and led them into the path of sin. Although these bands do not literally ask for the head of godly Spiritual leaders, they accomplish that spiritually and many times have more influence than godly Spiritual leaders in their cities, towns and nations.

The Arts and Entertainment world is not a world for the 'called' and 'anointed' to run from. Evil prevails when good men and women do nothing. If you are called into that world, take what is clean and godly and create pleasure for people, and leverage your influence with them by leading them into experiences with the person and principles of Jesus Christ.

An example of a godly Arts and Entertainment leader is no other than the former heavy weight champion of the world, George Foreman.

A HEAVY WEIGHT CAMPION FOR THE KINGDOM OF GOD:

George Edward Foreman was born to JD and Nancy Foreman on January 10, 1949, in the town of Marshall, Texas. As an impoverished youth, Foreman often bullied younger children and did not like getting up early for school. Foreman became a mugger and brawler on the hard streets of Houston's 5th Ward, by the age of 15.

George Foreman, from Thug to Boxer

Luckily, he was saved by Lyndon Johnson's Job Corps program which helped troubled kids. Foreman traveled to California where he met Job Corps Counselor and Boxing Coach, Doc Broaddus, who encouraged Foreman to become a fighter.

Once he began to train at the gym, Foreman rapidly established an impressive amateur record. The culmination of his amateur boxing career came at the 1968 Olympics in Mexico City, where he won a gold medal (25th Amateur Fight).

He got extra attention when he brandished an American flag after his win, "I wanted everyone in the world to know I was an American," he later explained, "and proud of the opportunity that I was given to do what I had done."

Foreman Becomes Heavyweight Champ

In 1969, Foreman turned professional. Within two years, Foreman was ranked the No. 1 challenger by the WBA and WBC; by 1972, Foreman's impressive record was 37 wins (most by knock- out) and no losses.

Foreman got his shot at the world heavyweight championship when he was scheduled to fight Joe Frazier in Kingston, Jamaica, on January 22, 1973. Frazier was the favorite going into the bout, but Foreman knocked him out in the second round. An unprecedented TV audience watched Foreman become the champ – the fight was HBO Boxing's first ever broadcast.

Foreman successfully defended his title twice. He beat Puerto Rican Heavyweight Champion, Jose Roman in 50 seconds, the shortest heavyweight championship match and he also beat Ken Norton (who had just beaten Muhammad Ali) in a mere two rounds. But when Foreman faced off against Ali himself in the summer of 1974, he went down.

The much-hyped "Rumble in the Jungle" in Kinshasa, Zaire, had been delayed due to an injury Foreman had suffered in training. Ali had spent the interim taunting Foreman relentlessly, which made him too angry and frustrated to stay focused.

Foreman Becomes Preacher then Champ Again!

After taking 1975 off, Foreman returned to boxing winning a number of fights before losing by decision to Jimmy Young in Puerto Rico in 1977. It was in his dressing room after the fight that Foreman had a religious experience; he then gave up Boxing and became a born-again Christian.

He was ordained a minister and began preaching in his hometown of Houston, Texas. In 1984, he founded the George Foreman Youth and Community Center, a non-denominational place for kids who need direction like he once did.

However, the George Foreman Center needed money to stay operational and by 1987, Foreman decided to return to Boxing to support it. Foreman proved his detractors wrong when he kept winning fights in his 40s and in 1991 he had a shot at the title, but lost to champ, Evander Holyfield by decision.

In 1994, however, Foreman took on the new champ Michael Moorer, and knocked him out in the 10th round. He became at 44, the oldest fighter ever to win the Heavyweight Crown and also the fighter with the most time between one world championship and the next. Foreman gave away his titles in 1995 after defending them against Axel Schultz and refusing a rematch.

George Foreman & the Lean Mean Grilling Machine

By the time Foreman retired from Boxing (again) in 1999, he was well on his way to a second career as a businessman. Since the early 1990s, Foreman had discovered his talent for salesmanship, and by the end of the decade he was making millions from infomercials marketing. The George Foreman Lean Mean Grilling Machine has sold over 100 million units to date.

George has also spent over a decade promoting Meineke Car Care Centers and has grown the business to over 1000 franchises. George has now successfully launched a line of environmentally safe cleaning products, an exclusive line of personal care products, a health shake called George Foreman's Life Shake, a prescription shoe for diabetics to prevent amputations, a restaurant franchise called UFood Grille, 10 books, and the list continues to build. (www.georgeforeman.com).

The Charge
If you are called to the sphere of Arts and Entrainment leadership, what a privilege. Your sphere is the most influential it has ever been and has now become the driver of much of popular culture.

Understand the greatness of your calling and intentionally influence your nation with your worth, lifestyle and kingdom of God values message.

End Notes

1. Beetles: Wikipedia

2. George Foreman www.georgeforemen.com

CHAPTER FIFTEEN

THE DYNAMICS OF ORGANIZATIONAL LEADERSHIP

Organizational Leadership influences nations by guiding the organization of human resources, financial resources and material resources to execute clearly defined missions and goals.

Organizations are built because individual visionaries have a solution that cannot be served by them alone. They are compelled to organize people, financial and material resources in a structured and strategic way to accomplish their visions. This type of leadership is the art of deploying the skills, character and passion of people while maximizing financial and material resources, to create goods and services that add value to humanity. This is the glory of this sphere of leadership.

I have discovered by observation and revelation that the organizational leadership gift is a three-legged stool.

- The first leg of the stool is an innate gift to organize human, financial and material resources to execute a vision.

- The second leg of the stool is an innate passion for a particular industry.

The innate passion in you, defines the industry that your organizational gift must be used in, e.g., there are those who have an innate passion for media, however, they are not called to be a journalist, movie star or a media leader.

They are called to be an organizational leader within the media industry and organize human and financial and material resources to execute media-driven missions and goals.

Another person with a similar leadership gift may have a passion for social organizations or political organizations and is therefore called to use their organizational gift to advance a social or political agenda.

There are people also who are called to work in the church world and use their organizational leadership skills to advance a church agenda.

Failing to recognize this would usually cause an organizational leader to love what they do, but not enjoy who they are doing it for, because they are doing the right thing in the wrong place.

So placement is very important and organizational leaders are needed in the church, government, legal, business, technology, educational, social, arts, entertainment, banking, and finance world. If you are called to be an organizational leader, take the time to find out where your gift should be placed.

- The third aspect is Leadership Intelligence. There are different types of Genetic Intelligence that produce different kinds of leaders, which include; strategic, tactical, logistical, and diplomatic leaders. Strategic leaders excel at making strategic decisions, tactical leaders excel in making tactical decisions, logistical leaders excel in making logistical decisions and diplomatic leaders excel in developing and mediating with people.

Strategic Decision Making

Strategy is a series of sequential steps that takes you from your present reality to your desired future. It sets the vision course and creates the path for the organization. It examines its internal and external obstacles and in the business arena evaluates the impact of the competition. Strategic decision-making must be made at the helm of successful companies. An effective decision making model has strategy that has been crafted from the top.

Tactical Decision Making

Tactics are the art of making moves to better one's position in the present, whether these moves are marketing a product, positioning a service within a market, creating a great presentation or successfully promoting a product. Defining the aspects of your organization's activities that are tactical and placing your best tactical leaders, managers and implementers in those roles will enhance your organization. The best sales people are usually tactical.

Logistical Decision Making

Logistics is the procurement, distribution service, and management of materials and resources. It is a vital part of any organization. In an army, the generals and war planners create the strategy. The logistical leaders move materials and resources in an organized way to make the strategy happen. The tactical commanders implement the war plan and in the heat of conflict make moves to better their position. Logistical operations cover areas like office administration, accounting and any position related to the management of resources.

Diplomatic or People Development Decision Making

Diplomacy and people development are the backbone of any great organization because they manage materials and lead people. Trying to manage people is an impossible task. It is not an effective approach as no individual person is identical and every person requires a slightly different approach to ignite their passion and deploy their skills effectively. Diplomatic people make your best human resource consultants and people developers in your organization. They have an innate wisdom to unleash potential in people, mediate and bring harmony among different people.

Every Organizational leader will have a primary strength in one of these four areas and a secondary strength so take the time to discover the areas of your strength. For more on this you can read my book, *'The Gift of Organizational Leadership.'*

Let's look at Nehemiah, one of the greatest organizational leaders in the Bible.

Nehemiah: An organizational Leader that changed a Nation

"So I came to Jerusalem and was there three days. Then I arose in the night, I and a few men with me; I told no one what my God had put in my heart to do at Jerusalem; nor was there any animal with me, except the one on which I rode. And I went out by night through the Valley Gate to the Serpent Well and the Refuse Gate, and viewed the walls of Jerusalem which were broken down and its gates which were burned with fire. Then I went on to the Fountain Gate and to the King's Pool, but there was no room for the animal under me to pass. So I went up in the night by the valley, and viewed the wall; then I turned back and entered by the Valley Gate, and so returned. And the officials did not know where I had gone or what I had done; I had not yet told the Jews, the priests, the nobles, the officials, or the others who did the work. Then I said to them, "You see the distress that we are in, how Jerusalem lies waste, and its gates are burned with fire. Come and let us build the wall of Jerusalem, that we may no longer be a reproach." And I told them of the hand of my God which had been good upon me, and also of the king's words that he had spoken to me. So they said, "Let us rise up and build." Then they set their hands to this good work (Nehemiah 2:11 -18)."

The three legged stool of the organizational leadership gift was manifested in the life of Nehemiah as follows:

1. He had a strong gift as he was able to organize human, financial and material resources to rebuild the walls of Jerusalem in a hostile environment in record time.

2. When he is introduced in the Scriptures, he is working in a political environment as a cup bearer to the king. He then asked the king if he could go on an assignment and use his gifts to organize the rebuilding of the walls of Jerusalem under the political authority of the king.

    The king agreed and Nehemiah was able to carry out his life's work and become the governor of the city. He was not a politician as he did not lobby or campaign for political office. He was an organizational leader working in a political and governmental establishment.

3. His primary intelligence was very logistical as he was able to execute a logistical miracle by managing resources and deploying people to build the walls of Jerusalem. His secondary intelligence was tactical as he was very wise in leveraging his influence with the king and placing himself in the best possible position to rebuild the walls of Jerusalem. He truly was an outstanding organizational leader.

Logistical Task Masters from Hell

Satan also has organizational leaders that he depends upon and they run his organization enterprises and movements with ruthless efficiency and effectiveness. An example of this are the taskmasters of Egypt in Exodus 1:11:

"Therefore, they did set over them taskmasters to afflict them with their burdens. And they built for Pharaoh treasure cities, Pithom and Raamses."

We can see from the scriptures that the task masters were very efficient by the treasure cities which were built for Pharaoh.

The Charge

Organizational leaders turn imagination to vision, vision to goals, goals to a plan, a plan to a dream team, a dream team into executing the plan, executing the plans to achieve goals and achieved goals to fulfilled vision.

If you are called to the sphere of organizational leadership, then cherish and celebrate this precious gift, find out where it should be placed, discover the intelligence you have, and add value to your world.

Discovering Your Leadership Assignment

CHAPTER SIXTEEN

STEPS TO DISCOVER AND FULFILL YOUR LEADERSHIP ASSIGNMENT

These Twelve Spheres of Leadership reveal the areas where God plans to position you. There are some people that are called and have an assignment to operate in one sphere of leadership. There are some that operate in two or three spheres of leadership, and very few that would operate in four and above.

This is because in order to maximize your impact you need to specialize. Jesus, who was the most impactful man in the history of the world operated only in one sphere of leadership and that was 'Spiritual Leadership.' The three spheres of leadership in which I operate are Spiritual, Media and Philosophic Leadership.

I will now share with you some steps to help you discern the type of leader that you are called to be.

Every creature that God created was given innate passion, innate wisdom, and innate energy. Fish have an innate passion to swim and do not have a passion to walk, because walking is not part of their design. They also have an innate wisdom to swim and they do not need to take swimming classes as the ability to swim is on the inside of them. They are very skillful as they swim throughout the sea and do not need to take skill development courses. They are also energized as they swim since swimming brings them pleasure.

This is true for all animals who operate primarily by instinct and therefore stay true to their identity. The only exception to this in the animal kingdom is when you have an animal that has been trained by humans and they acquire passion and skills that do not reflect their identity such as an elephant playing football with his trunk at a circus.
These elephants have been confused by humans.

Human beings, because we are made in the image of God, can live out of their true authentic identity or overrule it with their thoughts and ideas. A man can decide that he is going to change his gender and become a woman. A person that was born to preach and teach can decide that he is going to overrule his innate passion, wisdom and energy and become a race car driver which would normally end up in a disaster.

INNATE PASSION

Passion is a strong emotion that compels you to action. Within you, there is an innate passion to contribute something to the world. This is different from an acquired passion. When I was growing up, I felt an innate passion to preach the Word of God and to study philosophies. However, I saw no successful model of this in my environment and therefore decided to be an engineer and then a businessman which did not work, because those endeavors' took me out of the plans and purposes of God for my life.

Due to the revelation from God, I later decided to live in my innate passion which is to represent a move of God in wisdom and power that takes people and nations from bondage to greatest

What do you have innate passion to contribute, add and serve to people as a solution?

_____

_____

_____

_____

_____

INNATE WISDOM

Wisdom is thinking thoughts, applying principles and taking steps to create what you desire. What you have innate wisdom in, you can always create. I have an innate wisdom to minister miracles to people and create curricula that release greatness in people. I do not have an innate wisdom to sing and hit notes. After taking singing lessons for six months, my vocal music teacher told me that he did not think I would have a career as a singer, because after my voice had broken, the more I tried to sing and hit the notes, the worse I sounded.

What areas of life and what spheres of leadership do you have innate wisdom in?

_____

_____

_____

_____

_____

INNATE ENERGY

Doing what you were born to do energizes you. When I was in engineering class, my brain started to malfunction. There was a fog over it, but when I started studying leadership, philosophy and theology, my brain was energized.

What tasks do you do that energize you?

_____

_____

_____

_____

Use the answers that you have written down to these three questions to discern the leadership spheres you are called to function in and your leadership assignment.

God has built in you a storehouse of innate energy to use the innate wisdom He has given you to fulfill a purpose that you are innately passionate about.

CHAPTER SEVENTEEN

I SEE A LEADERSHIP MOVEMENT ARISING

What would your Nation look like if Godly leaders arise in the 12 Spheres of Leadership?

When the church arises out of its slumber and becomes light, Godly leaders will emerge from the womb of the church and bring transformation to the culture of each of the 12 Spheres of Leadership in your nation

When the church arises out of its slumber and becomes salt, Godly leaders will emerge from the womb of the church and preserve the divine in the culture of each of the 12 Spheres of Leadership in your nation

When this happens what is the real outcome in nations and do we have examples? The answer is a resounding yes. Let's take a deeper look

Luke 10:10-16 KJV, "But into whatsoever city ye enter, and they receive you not, go your ways out into the streets of the same, and say, (11) Even the very dust of your city, which cleaveth on us, we do wipe off against you: notwithstanding be ye sure of this, that the kingdom of God is come nigh unto you. (12) But I say unto you, that it shall be more tolerable in that day for Sodom, than for that city. (13) Woe unto thee, Chorazin! woe unto thee, Bethsaida! for if the mighty works had been done in Tyre and Sidon, which have been done in you, they had a great while ago repented, sitting in sackcloth and ashes. (14) But it shall be more tolerable for Tyre and Sidon at the judgment, than for you. (15) And thou, Capernaum, which art exalted to heaven, shalt be thrust down to hell. (16) He that heareth you heareth me; and he that despiseth you despiseth me; and he that despiseth me despiseth him that sent me."

This scripture teaches us that not only will people be judged on the Day of Judgement but cities and nations will also be judged. Sodom, Chorazin Bethsaida, Capernaum, Tyre and Sidon were not individuals but territories that defiled their God given greatness and buried the glory and honour that God deposited in them corporately. They became *evil and adulterous territories.*

Mat 12:39-42 KJV, "But he answered and said unto them, An evil and adulterous generation seeketh after a sign; and there shall no sign be given to it, but the sign of the prophet Jonas: (40) For as Jonas was three days and three nights in the whale's belly; so shall the Son of man be three days and three nights in the heart of the earth. (41) The men of Nineveh shall rise in judgment with this generation, and shall condemn it: because they repented at the preaching of Jonas; and, behold, a greater than Jonas is here. (42) The queen of the south shall rise up in the judgment with this generation, and shall condemn it: for she came from the uttermost parts of the earth to hear the wisdom of Solomon; and, behold, a greater than Solomon is here."

What does an evil and adulterous nation look like?

In understanding this scripture, you must understand that the Word of

God has two aspects. It reveals the person of God and the Principles or philosophy of God.

A person can walk in the principles and philosophy of God like integrity, giving, wealth creation, service and compassion and not know the person of God as Lord and Savior.

On the other hand, a person can know the person of God and violate many of the principles and philosophy of God in their daily lives.

Does this also applies to nations?

Moses introduced the person and philosophy of God to Israel. There are generations in nations like the multitude of adult Israelites that left Egypt that knew the God of Abraham, Isaac and Jacob yet rebelled against his philosophies and principles. There are also nations that follow his philosophies like Persia under Cyrus that do not have a great revelation of the God of the Heavens and the Earth

When a Nation is adulterous, a critical mass of its population abandons the worship of the Almighty God.

When it is evil, its culture and philosophies in the 12 Spheres of Leadership are the product of demons.

Isaiah 59:14-15, "*Justice is turned back, And righteousness stands afar off; For truth is fallen in the street, And equity cannot enter. So truth fails, And he who departs from evil makes himself a prey. Then the Lord saw it, and it displeased Him That there was no justice.*"

Some nations like Japan have a culture full of divine principles but do not have a great revelation of Jesus Chris as Savior. They are adulterous.

Some nations the United Kingdom have had great outpouring of God and are now embracing a culture that is against Gods principles and values. It actually has a foreign policy of promoting and forcing the same sex agenda to it commonwealth nations. That culture is evil.

What is the outcome when a nation combines both what is evil and adulterous? If God does not find a leader to anoint to bring reformation, national extinction is usually certain.

How does God judge nations?

1. God judge's nations by evaluating each successive generation and giving it the harvest they are due.

   Scriptural Examples
   A. The first generation of Israel that came out of Egypt was so evil and in the sight of God that if it was not for the intercession of Moses they would have all being wipeout and a greater nation created with Moses as the Father.

   Numbers14: 10 -24, "And all the congregation said to stone them with stones. Now the glory of the Lord appeared in the tabernacle of meeting before all the children of Israel. Then the Lord said to Moses: How long will these people reject Me? And how long will they not believe Me, with all the signs which I have performed among them? I will strike them with the pestilence and disinherit them, and I will make of you a nation greater and mightier than they. And Moses said to the Lord: Then the Egyptians will hear it, for by Your might You brought these people up from among them, and they will tell it to the inhabitants of this land. They have heard that You, Lord, are among these people; that You, Lord, are seen face to face and Your cloud stands above them, and You go before them in a pillar of cloud by day and in a pillar of fire by night. Now if You kill these people as one man, then the nations which have heard of Your fame will speak, saying, 'Because the Lord was not able to bring this people to the land which He swore to give them, therefore He killed them in the wilderness.' And now, I pray, let the power of my Lord be great, just as You have spoken, saying, 'The Lord is longsuffering and abundant in mercy, forgiving iniquity and transgression; but He by no means clears the guilty, visiting the iniquity of the fathers on the children to the third and fourth generation.' Pardon the iniquity of this people, I pray, according to the greatness of Your mercy, just as You have forgiven this people, from Egypt even until now. Then the Lord said: "I have pardoned, according to your word; but truly, as I live, all the earth shall be filled with the glory of the Lord-- because all these men who have seen My glory and the signs which I did in Egypt and in the wilderness, and have put Me to the test now these ten times, and have not heeded My voice, they certainly shall not see the land of which I swore to their fathers, nor shall any of those who rejected Me see it."

B. David lead Israel into to an era of worship of God, prosperity, national greatness and stability.

Act 13:36 KJV, *"For David, after he had served his own generation by the will of God, fell on sleep, and was laid unto his fathers, and saw corruption:"*

2. Some generations become so adulterous and evil without transformational leadership that he judges them with extinction through either war, famine and calamity or all three.

1 Kings 8:33, "When thy people Israel be smitten down before the enemy, because they have sinned against thee,"

1Kings 8:35 "When heaven is shut up, and there is no rain, because they have sinned against thee;"

1 Kings 8:37, "If there be in the land famine, if there be pestilence, blasting, mildew, locust, or if there be caterpiller; if their enemy besiege them in the land of their cities; whatsoever plague, whatsoever sickness there be;"

3. The leaders of a generation in a nation will determine its Judgement before God.

What this means is that if a critical mass of leaders from the church do not take generational responsibility in your nation, the outcome will be an adulterous and evil generation. Let it not be said that you refused to be salt and light in your nation.

What does a nation look like that has a critical mass of leaders ? Who are vessels of the Kingdom of God ideas and solutions?

It is a nation that has a dominant culture of personal responsibility, pursuit of happiness, freedom, strong traditional families, wealth creation, government for the people, rule of law, social justice, economic dignity, security, global relevance and has an honor of the things of God. This is not a perfect nation where very one is saved it is a nation that is global asset, serves God given solutions to the world and honors the people and things of God.

It was Israel under David. Israel under Joshua. America in the glory years before the Secular Progressives took over the Judicial, Political, Arts and Entertainment, Media and Entrepreneurial spheres. And South Korea in the 21st Century. All were awed at, respected and accomplished great things, even in challenging periods.

There are many examples in history of righteous generations in nations. The question however, is what are you going to do in your generation. I and my house have chosen like David to serve our generation by the will of God. What about you?

Luke 21:29-32 KJV, "And he spake to them a parable; Behold the fig tree, and all the trees; When they now shoot forth, ye see and know of your own selves that summer is now nigh at hand. So likewise ye, when ye see these things come to pass, know ye that the kingdom of God is nigh at hand. Verily I say unto you, This generation shall not pass away, till all be fulfilled."

There is a last generation in every nation that is not extinct that will see the unfolding of the second coming of Christ. My prayer is that because of the Godly leaders of the generation, your nation is not found evil and adulterous.

The Power of One Transformational Leader

*Ezekiel 22:23-31 KJV, "And the word of the LORD came unto me, saying, Son of man, say unto her, Thou art the land that is not cleansed, nor rained upon in the day of indignation. There is a conspiracy of her prophets in the midst thereof, like a roaring lion ravening the prey; they have devoured souls; they have taken the treasure and precious things; they have made her many widows in the midst thereof. Her priests have violated my law, and have profaned mine holy things: they have put no difference between the holy and profane, neither have they shewed difference between the unclean and the clean, and have hid their eyes from my sabbaths, and I am profaned among them. Her princes in the midst thereof are like wolves ravening the prey, to shed blood, and to destroy souls, to get dishonest gain. And her prophets have daubed them with untempered morter, seeing vanity, and divining lies unto them, saying, Thus saith the Lord GOD, when the LORD hath not spoken. The people of the land have used oppression, and exercised robbery, and have vexed the poor and needy: yea, they have oppressed the stranger wrongfully. **And I sought for a man among them, that should make up the hedge, and stand in the gap before me for the land, that I should not destroy it: but I found none.** Therefore have I poured out mine indignation upon them; I have consumed them with the fire of my wrath: their own way have I recompensed upon their heads, saith the Lord GOD."*

What a dire situation:

The sphere of spiritual leadership is defiled by vain self-serving prophets and priests.

The political leaders are lack thereof *are* like wolves ravening the prey.

The social institutions oppressed the stranger wrongfully and not defended the poor and needy.

The judiciary leaders have been complicit as oppression and robbery have vexed the poor and needy.

God's answer? It is one transformational leader. One man or woman who can influence the nation from their spheres of assignment. One man or woman through whom the kingdom of God will come in ideas and solutions.

Is that person YOU!

The Lord has given me a mandate to take wisdom to visionaries so that 2 million of them will execute divine assignments in the 12 Spheres of Leadership.

It is not by mere coincidence that you are reading this book. You have been handpicked and selected to be a part of a movement of leaders that will use their giftings to influence their nations for God, like Esther, Daniel, Nehemiah, Moses and David just to name a few. All things are possible with the help of the Holy Spirit.

Prayer to Reveal My Gifts and Life Mission

Father in the name of Jesus Christ according to Psalms 8:4-5 , *"What is man that you take notice of him, or the son of man that you pay attention to him? You made him a little less than divine, but you crowned him with glory and honor."*

- I ask that you anoint my eyes with eye salve so that I see my glory and honor.
- I ask that you teach me about my gifts and life's mission.

- Reveal to me every wrong step in my life that takes me away from wearing my crown of gifts and life mission.
- Every Satanic force that has created a weapon against me wearing my glory gifts and honorable life mission I cast you out and destroy you by the power of the Holy Ghost in Jesus name. (Prayer fervently)

Prayer to Reveal the Spheres of Leadership I Was Born to Influence in This Season of My Life

Father, I come before the Throne of Grace with boldness and ask that you reveal the spheres of leadership that my gifts and life mission are supposed to function in.

- Every obstacle to this revelation be destroyed by fire in Jesus name.
- Oh Holy Spirit manifest yourself to me as the Spirit of Counsel like you did to Job when he said: (Job 29:2-4 KJV) *"Oh that I were as in months past, as in the days when God preserved me; When his candle shined upon my head, and when by his light I walked through darkness; As I was in the days of my youth, when the secret cousel of God was upon my tabernacle;"*
- Bring me out of obscurity by your favor and secret counsel like you did David and I will *"Be not as the horse, or as the mule, which have no understanding: whose mouth must be held in with bit and bridle, lest they come near unto thee (Psalms 32:9)"*.
- I will walk in rhythm with your times and seasons for my life as Amos 3:3 declares, *"Can two walk together, except they be agreed?"*
- I am yours God, I belong to you Father of glory. Lead me into paths of righteousness and greatness. (Prayer fervently)

Prayer to bring out the Greatness in you

My Heavenly Father your word says that (1Ch 29:11-12 KJV) *"Thine, O LORD, is the greatness, and the power, and the glory, and the victory, and the majesty: for all that is in the heaven and in the earth is thine; thine is the kingdom, O LORD, and thou art exalted as head above all. Both riches and honour come of thee, and thou reignest over all; and in thine hand is power and might; and in thine hand it is to make great, and to give strength unto all."*

- Anoint me to rise to the greatness version of me.
- I am weak and have no strength but I now know the true strength comes from you.
- Strengthen me O; God of Angel Armies to take my Jericho and territory
- Grant me honor and more than enough money for my life mission in Jesus Christ name
- I praise You and worship for you are my Source for my strengths, honor, riches and greatness comes from only you
  (Praise God fervently)

I declare that the Spirit of wisdom and revelation in the knowledge of your assignment and the leadership sphere to which you were called comes upon you, and you arise out of any bondages that maybe imprisoning the greatest version of yourself and represent God in the sphere of your calling.

Be blessed,

Bishop Andre Thomas

OTHER BOOKS BY ANDRE THOMAS

1. The Organizational Visionary
2. The Gift of Political Leadership
3. The 12 Spheres of Leadership
4. Unlock Your Greatness (A Young Leaders' Handbook)
5. Discovering Me
6. Uncommon Men and Distinguished Women
7. Coaching People into the 12 Spheres of Leadership
8. Seven Principles of Commonwealth Leadership
9. Discovering your Leadership Assignment
10. Preparing for your Leadership Assignment
11. Executing your Leadership Assignment
12. I Am a Leader (Inspiring Greatness in Kids)
13. The Entrepreneurial Visionary
14. The Social Visionary
15. From Brokenness to Wholeness

ABOUT THE 12 SPHERES OF LEADERSHIP MOVEMENT

Purpose
To raise up a global movement of the 12 types of leaders that shape the destinies of nations.

Our Mission
To take wisdom to visionaries so that two million of them will execute divine assignments in the 12 spheres of leadership

OUR METHODS

Conferences
To form strategic partnerships with key national leaders to hold 12 Spheres of Leadership conferences, events and speaking engagements.

Media and Communication

1.   To create media programs and a media platform to distribute 12 Spheres of Leadership content to the world.

2.   To communicate monthly to our partners through 'Leadership Fuel,' a monthly audio teaching and news digest.

Books

To write, publish and distribute books that influence and empower leaders globally to execute divine assignments in the 12 spheres of leadership.

How can your church, town, city or nation be transformed by the 12 Spheres of Leadership Movement?

There are four different events that we conduct:

1.   LEADERSHIP WISDOM EXPLOSION

An event where:

- The biblical wisdom of the 12 Spheres of Leadership is imparted to equip the saints and to shape the destinies of their nations.

- Visionaries are refreshed by the Holy Spirit.

- This event can also be customized to focus on specific spheres of leadership.

2.   ANOINTING REVIVAL

An event where:
- A fresh anointing is imparted to people individually and enmasse to unlock their God-given greatness.

- The delivering and healing power of God is also administered to set people free from all bondage.

3.   ANOINTING AND WISDOM CONFERENCE

This event features the best of Anointing Revival and Leadership Explosion Event in one conference that catapults the saints into higher dimensions of leadership, breakthrough, freedom, influence and impact.

4.   APEX MINISTERS CONFERENCE

An event that equips ministers of the Gospel with wisdom and power so that they will manifest the greatest of their callings to the territories they are assigned.

www.12slm.org